RA

GU

t

BIRMINGHAM

and the

BLACK COUNTRY

MIKE PARKER

HARRAP
LONDON

First published in Great Britain 1991
by HARRAP BOOKS Ltd
Chelsea House, 26 Market Square,
Bromley, Kent BR1 1NA

ISBN 0 245-60273-9

Designed by Roger King Graphic Studios.
Printed in Great Britain by
Guernsey Press

PREFACE & ACKNOWLEDGEMENTS

Preface

RAW is about looking at places with a keen, sometimes cynical, often irreverent eye. Many guide books over-rely on pictures of misty churchyards at sunrise and sun-dappled glades superimposed with the ramblings of some 'local' poet. ***RAW*** celebrates the diversity of the cities and regions of the British Isles, and believes that London and the south-east of England are not the last word in culture, excitement and vitality.

This guide should help you sort out the rhetoric from the reality, and to learn to look at the West Midlands in a new way. Some things mentioned may well take a dash of perseverance to find and appreciate; you may blatantly disagree with some of the opinions expressed. If so, then tell us. But we hope that, if you do bother to do more than just scratch the surface, you will agree that this is a very exciting time to be part of the West Midlands. Enjoy!

Acknowledgements

MAPS

Midline BR map (page 7) reproduced by kind permission of Centro.

Maps on pages 6, 8, 9, 10 by Roger King Graphic Studios based on maps from DE ROUCK Cartography.

CONTRIBUTORS

Jane Dawson
Ruth Smith
Sue Bedwell
Eric Macneil
Ian Garner
Claire Hobbs
Katie Macneil
Carol Rowntree-Jones
Jon Woolcott

DEDICATION

To Dan Dan

CONTENTS

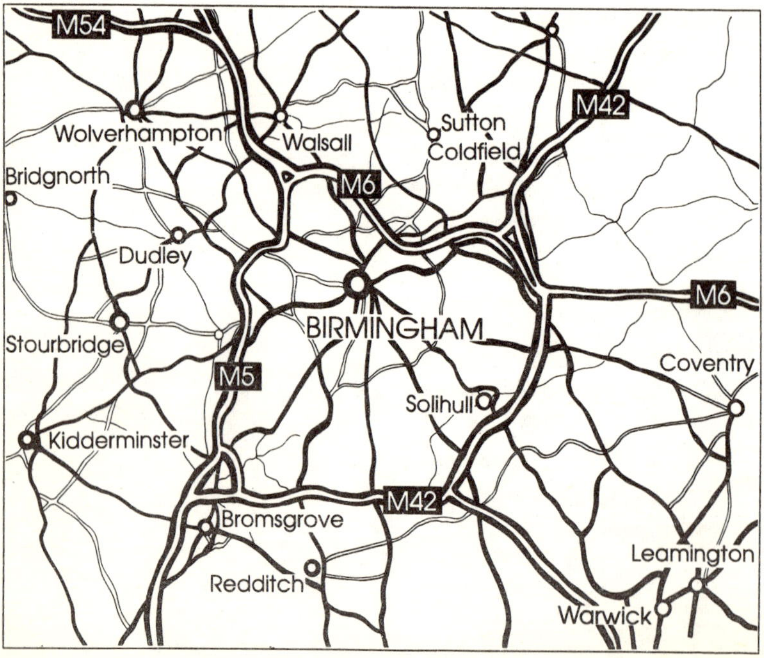

M54
Wolverhampton
Walsall
Sutton Coldfield
M42
Bridgnorth
M6
Dudley
M6
BIRMINGHAM
Stourbridge
M5
Coventry
Solihull
Kidderminster
M42
Bromsgrove
Leamington
Redditch
Warwick

MIDLINE BR

Train Service Guide numbers
Free car parking
Other car parking
National Exhibition Centre
Direct access to airport
Severn Valley Railway
© 1990 British Railways Board
Crewe, Stoke
Chester Mid Wales
Stafford
Rugeley
Penkridge
Shrewsbury
Wellington Telford West
Oakengates
Telford Central
Shifnal
Cosford
Albrighton
Codsall
Bilbrook
WOLVERHAMPTON
Coseley
Tipton
Dudley Port
Sandwell & Dudley
Smethwick Rolfe Street
SNOW HILL
NEW STREET
Hednesford
Cannock
Landywood
Broad Lane
Bloxwich
Walsall
Bescot
Tame Bridge
Hamstead
Perry Barr
Witton
Lichfield Trent Valley
Lichfield City
Shenstone
Blake Street
Butlers Lane
Four Oaks
Sutton Coldfield
Wylde Green
Chester Road
Erdington
Gravelly Hill
Aston
Duddeston
Tamworth
Burton Derby
Polesworth
Wilnecote
Atherstone
Nuneaton
Leicester Nottingham
Water Orton
Smethwick West
Langley Green
Rowley Regis
Old Hill
Cradley Heath
Five Ways
University
Selly Oak
Bournville
Kings Norton
Northfield
Longbridge
Barnt Green
Alvechurch
Redditch
Bromsgrove
Stourbridge Town
Lye
Stourbridge Junction
Hagley
Blakedown
Kidderminster
Bridgnorth
Hartlebury
Droitwich Spa
Worcester Foregate Street
Worcester Shrub Hill
Great Malvern
Malvern Link
Pershore
Evesham
Hereford
Cheltenham
Oxford
Moor Street
Bordesley
Small Heath
Tyseley
Spring Road
Hall Green
Yardley Wood
Shirley
Whitlocks End
Wythall
Earlswood
The Lakes
Wood End
Danzey
Henley-in-Arden
Wootton Wawen
Wilmcote
Stratford-upon-Avon
Acocks Green
Olton
Solihull
Widney Manor
Dorridge
Lapworth
Claverdon
Hatton
Bearley
Warwick
Leamington Spa
Banbury, Oxford
Adderley Park
Stechford
Lea Hall
Marston Green
Birmingham International
Hampton-in-Arden
Berkswell
Tile Hill
Canley
COVENTRY
Bedworth
Rugby
Northampton

BIRMINGHAM CITY CENTRE

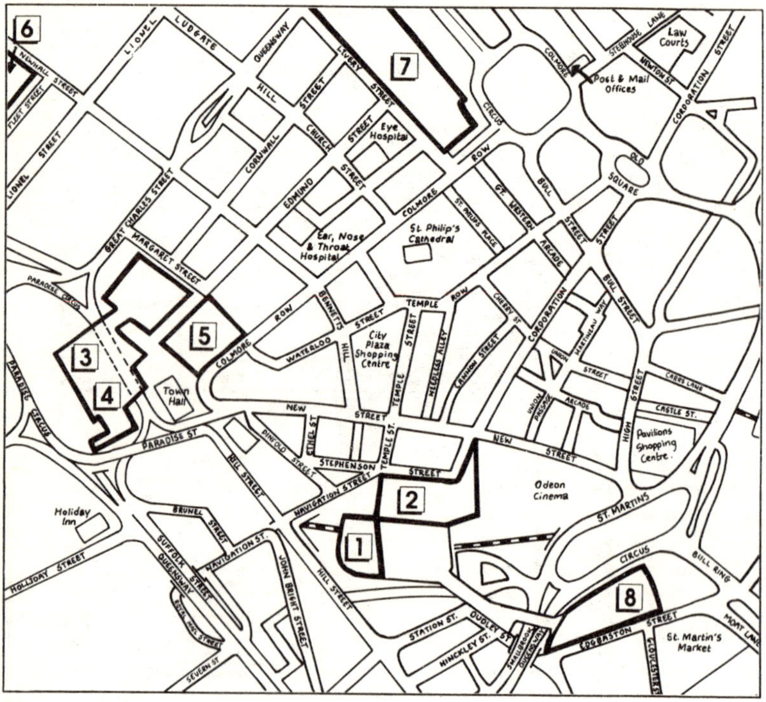

1 New Street Station

2 The Pallasades Shopping Centre

3 Central Library

4 School of Music

5 Council Offices

6 Museum of Science and Industry

7 Snow Hill Station

8 Bull Ring Shopping Centre

0 110 220 yards

0 100 200 metres

WOLVERHAMPTON TOWN CENTRE

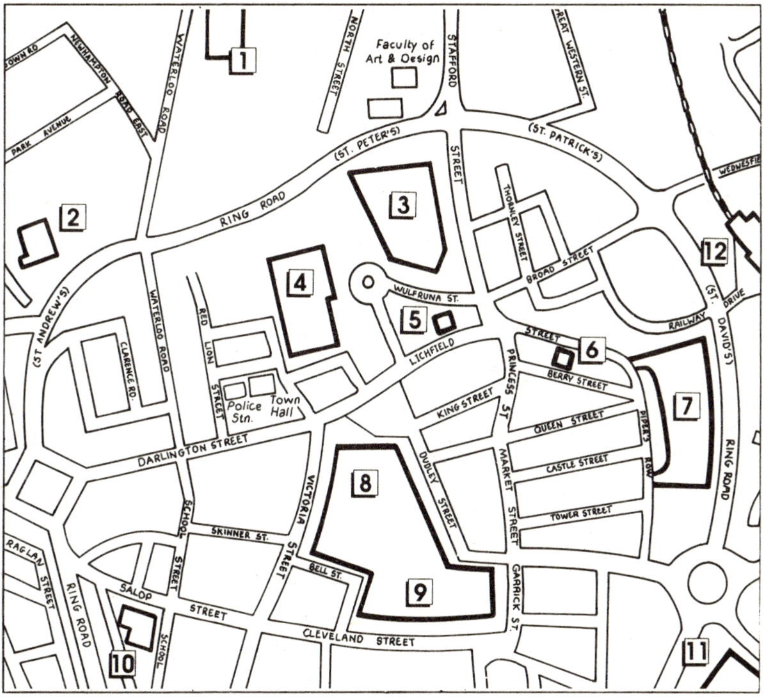

1 Wolverhampton Wanderers FC

2 Central Swimming Baths

3 Polytechnic

4 Civic Centre

5 Art Gallery

6 Grand Theatre

7 Bus Station

8 Mander Shopping Centre

9 Wulfrun Shopping Centre

10 Retail Market

11 Bus Garage

12 Railway Station

0 110 220 yards

0 100 200 metres

DUDLEY TOWN CENTRE

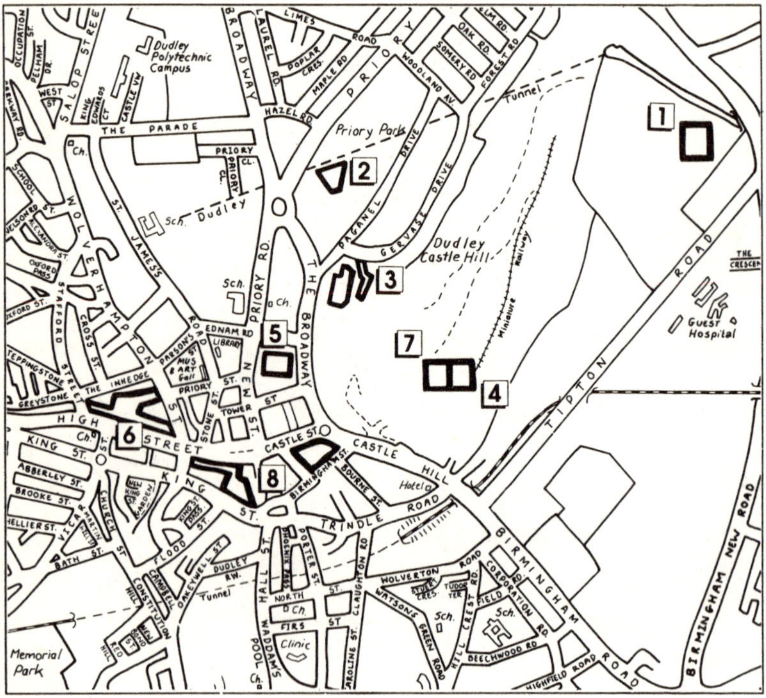

[1] Black Country Museum

[2] Priory Hall

[3] Technical College

[4] Dudley Castle ruins

[5] Town Hall

[6] Trident Centre

[7] Dudley Zoo

[8] Churchill Precinct and Bus Station

INTRODUCTION

Images of Birmingham and the Black Country vary enormously – usually dependent on just how well the person in question knows the area. It's a fascinating and diverse region that warrants a good deal of exploration, amply justifying the time spent in getting to know it. You should not get bored with the West Midlands very easily, for there is always something new, different or exciting, eager to be discovered.

However, people who have only scant or circumstantial knowledge of the area tend to scoff instinctively at the merest mention of it. If, for instance, a quick, cheap laugh is needed on a low-budget, low-humour sitcom, writers and producers often reach instinctively for the archetypal whining Brummie, thick as two short planks and with an accent that could curdle milk at forty paces.

This prejudice is periodically confirmed by those aggravatingly regular 'lifestyle' surveys, which put Birmingham at or near the bottom of virtually every league table in existence (occasionally coupled with its West Midland neighbours). The French magazine *Le Point*, in surveying European cities of over half a million people, adamantly plonked Birmingham in thirty-eighth position out of thirty-nine – beating only Istanbul. The British national press loved it – Brumophobia ran rampant. Apocryphal stories are systematically aired in the national media – did you know, they sneer, that Queen Victoria demanded that the blinds on her windows were drawn as her royal train passed between Wolverhampton and Birmingham? Chortle, chortle.

More recently, the untimely demise of the perennial Midland soap opera *Crossroads* was cause only for nationwide celebration. One can scarcely imagine the outrage if *Neighbours*, *EastEnders* or *Coronation Street* were to be given the chop. Naturally, the permanent 1970s feel, cardboard set (and acting) of *Crossroads* perhaps justified its end, but its setting in the suburbs of Birmingham only gave people greater licence to rejoice at its premature swansong. The West Midlands – the place, the people and, above all, the accent – are just not seen as being hip and trendy.

For instance, how many 'yoof' TV and radio presenters have a good solid Tipton twang or Digbeth drawl? It's an absolute bonus to have a Geordie, Scouse or Scottish accent, but the true sound of Brum and the Black Country is still seen as representing some evolutionary time-warp or cultural missing link.

Maybe this sounds a little over-defensive (if not verging on paranoid!). The West Midlands does have a great deal of which it is justly, if sometimes rather modestly, proud. Within the huge area stretching from Wolverhampton to Solihull, you are almost guaranteed to be able to find the shop, dance, people, pastime, pub, club, play, sport, politics or hairstyle that you're looking for. The area will never cease to surprise you, and the people will never fail to show you levels of courtesy and hospitality that have long since disappeared from the streets of other cities.

And also, retort the local authorities and revitalized tourist boards, what about the City of Birmingham Symphony Orchestra? The astounding success of the Black Country Museum? The relocation of Sadlers Wells Royal Ballet to Brum? The Super prix? The growing international success of the NEC and the burgeoning showpiece International Convention Centre? These are all, undoubtedly, successes of which the good people of the West Mids can be proud; but, it has to be asked, what do *they* get out of it? Is the West Midlands trying to run before it can walk, in putting on top-line international events while Birmingham city centre is still pretty dead on a Friday night?

The standard retort is that if the region markets itself for the international bigwigs and their megabucks, a trail of goodies will follow in their slipstream for the ordinary Midlander. Thus, to make the walk into the city centre a weeny bit more pleasant for ICC delegates, Birmingham City Council lowered the Inner Ring Road at Paradise Circus at vast cost. It's undoubtedly a great improvement for everyone: pity they didn't build the ICC in Handsworth, then....

One eternal problem is that the West Midlands simply is not far enough away from London. It's fine to be in Glasgow, Manchester, Newcastle or Cardiff – they're all seen as independent enough to sustain their own life and excitement. But New Street station is (sometimes) less than ninety minutes away from Euston – and that's just a little bit too close. Areas of the West Midlands and the surrounding rolling hills of Warwickshire and Worcestershire are fast becoming part of the outer London commuter belt, which ensures escalating house prices driving locals out and scaling down age-old amenities to week-end fripperies.

On the flip side of the same coin, it is remarkable that just over an hour from London finds you in such a markedly different region, with towns and cities notable for their homeliness and lack of pretension. So, Birmingham may not be as sophisticated or world-weary as London, or even Manchester, but it succeeds in maintaining a laconically modest and snug atmosphere that has quietly spawned one of the most diverse and exhilarating urban areas in Europe.

The metropolitan county of the West Midlands came into being in April 1974, created out of the desire to have one body overseeing the huge built-up sprawl that had once been a series of individual small towns and cities, each with their own staple industry. Chunks of Worcestershire, Staffordshire and Warwickshire were sliced off to form the new county – one that many people thought was synonymous merely with the city of Birmingham.

This is a big mistake. People from Dudley, Wolverhampton, Walsall, Sutton Coldfield or – heaven forbid! – Solihull are *not* Brummies. Those in Solihull hardly even acknowledge the fact that they live in the West Midlands – Solihull, Warwickshire sounds *so* much more appealing.

The West Midlands metropolitan county had a pathetically short life, finally shuffling off its mortal coil on 31 March 1986, victim of the government's abolition of the GLC and the six metropolitan counties. Needless to say, they all deserved to die, having had the most displeasingly consistent tendency to vote Labour! Responsibilities that belonged to the WMCC were divided between the grieving relatives: the seven district councils took on major areas such as education and social services, while many areas such as transport were stealthily secreted to some distantly accountable government quangos deep in the corridors of Westminster.

The heritage of the West Midlands is hand-in-glove with the Industrial Revolution. The towns of the region snowballed in size during the reign of Queen Victoria – Birmingham itself grew from a medium-sized industrial town into a vast regional metropolis, the 'city of 1,001 trades'. The epithet of the 'Black Country' emerged to describe the sooty, smoky, furnace-pocked land between Wolverhampton and Stourbridge.

Like many of its contemporaries in Scotland, Wales and the North of England, Birmingham was a fiercely proud, staunchly male municipal stronghold – described in 1890 by an American observer as 'the best-governed city in the world'. Due to the area's rapid growth, much of the development had been in providing low-cost slum housing with scant regard to hygiene or decent living conditions. Too many people still imagine this grime and soot that covered the West Midlands as a contemporary picture.

Throughout the twentieth century, the West Midlands has continued to grow in size and stature – and as a perennial source of cheap jokes and digs by outsiders. Not that the people of Birmingham and the Black

Country lack a sense of humour: it is, however, a rather laconic and self-deprecating humour that epitomizes much of the innocence and lack of self-esteem that so many West Midlanders suffer from. That, perhaps, is slowly changing, as the region comes to terms with its depleted manufacturing sector and its new role in other industries and the services.

Today's West Midlands is a richly diverse and multicultural society. The wealth of excellent and very reasonable restaurants and cafés is but one testimony to this, as is the variety of cultural and arts events, shops, architecture and daily encounters. One cannot brush aside events such as the disturbances in Handsworth in the early eighties, but it is important to put these in context and to recognize the work that has been done to bridge the gaps that resulted in such a tragically alienated section of society. Thankfully, the evil of racism, which became the dominant issue in the Smethwick by-election as recently as the mid-1960s, is now nowhere near such a force.

The region is rapidly changing, and to live here is to be part of a culture that is once again beginning to assert itself and its indomitable spirit. This acceleration is happening on many different levels and at very many varied speeds: The work of Birmingham City Council in its international aspirations (exemplified in the city's unsuccessful Olympic bid for the 1992 games, which elicited no more than outright sneers from the national media); the metamorphosis of the Black Country into an unlikely but fascinating and proud tourist attraction; the contentious inner-city regeneration work in the massive Heartlands project, right through to the fast-burgeoning community ventures, land and building reclamation and the oft-quoted 'people power', all of which are gathering unstoppable momentum in the area.

There is a tangible feeling of renewal in the air – as, one might argue, there would have to be to stop the conurbation curling up and dying. The recession of the early 1980s thwacked the West Midlands right where it hurts: over one-third of the region's engineering businesses went into liquidation between 1979 and 1983. The fight back had to happen. And, most people would agree, it is. We can only hope that the lessons have been learned from the last period of rebuilding mania that swept the region in the 1960s, leaving decimated town and city centres (especially Birmingham) in its concrete wake.

1. ORIENTATION

Travel and Transport

Public transport is fairly comprehensive and easy to follow. This may well prove difficult to believe when you've been shivering at a bus stop for half an hour in the vain hope of the arrival of a blue-and-silver beastie. But, surely, you cry, that's the same everywhere? Well, yes – but the snag here is that the buses are, for most areas, the only form of public transport around.

In the post-war years, when many cities were rebuilding their shattered centres and infrastructure, talk of a tube system was heard in the council chambers of the area. But, while the wise councillors of Glasgow, Liverpool and Newcastle invested in speedy local transit services, the thrifty burghers of Brum shelved project after project on the grounds of cost. Now **Centro** (the trendy new name of the West Midland Passenger Transport Executive) is finally giving the go-ahead to thrust the region into the third millennium with an electric-tram-style system. It will be known as the **Midland Metro**, and the first line is due to open between Wolverhampton, Birmingham and the NEC in the next few years. Others will follow, but it would seem that they may well be covering routes, like the first one, already well served by rail links. But until – and maybe even when – this happens, the West Midlands will remain as woefully slow in its public-transport network on the roads as most other major conurbations.

LOCAL TRAVEL

Local Trains – Midline

Although there is a fairly good local rail network, it converges like the spokes of a wheel on to the city centre of Birmingham – mainly at New Street station, although Stratford, Leamington and Warwick trains go from the new-look Snow Hill and Moor Street stations, which means that changing trains can involve a good hike across the city centre.

There have been no new rail lines built this century in the West Midlands, so all rail connections tend to link places that were identifiable and autonomous towns in their own right back in the days of good Queen Vic. Added to this, in common with everywhere else, a great many lines were axed in the myopic zeal of the Beeching cuts – lines that nowadays would undoubtedly be very well used and viable.

The map on page 7 shows the lines and stations still in operation. Services are generally quite reliable, although weekend trains are often sketchy (especially on Sundays, when some lines are shut altogether). Delays – as anywhere on British 'We're getting there' Rail – are quite commonplace, especially on local-rush hour trains speeding the commuting hordes back to their Barratt mock-Tudor executive homes in Sutton Coldfield Borders (i.e. next to Spaghetti Junction).

The Midline services come into their own for getting out of the smog into the surrounding towns and villages. Easy to reach this way are Shrewsbury, Lichfield, Worcester, the Malvern Hills, Warwick, Leamington, Coventry, Telford and Ironbridge, the Severn Valley Railway and, of course, Bardsville UK, Stratford-upon-Tourist. Perhaps you may prefer the idea of getting some gentle walking and a few country pubs under your urbanized belt. If so, there are some very accessible, seemingly remote rural stations within easy reach. Some fine trips out are listed below.

- **Lapworth** or **Hatton** stations on the Leamington line, for fine strolls and pubs along the Grand Union Canal. Both Packwood House and Baddesley Clinton stately homes are about a mile from Lapworth station.
- **Wilmcote** (for Mary Arden's house and the Stratford Canal), **Wootten Wawen**, **Earlswood** and **The Lakes** (for Clowes Wood and, not surprisingly, Earlswood Lakes) on the Stratford line.
- **Barnt Green** for the back end of the ever-popular Lickey Hills on the Bromsgrove or Redditch lines.
- **Hagley** for Hagley Hall and the beautiful Clent Hills, and Blakedown on the Kidderminster line.
- **Hednesford**, at the end of the line beyond Walsall, for the Rawnsley Hills on the edge of the great Cannock Chase Forest.

For information on these services, pick up Midline's free timetable (which includes Inter-City times to London), or ring BR on one of these numbers:

Birmingham	021-643 2711 (24 hours)
Coventry	0203-555211
Gloucester	0452-29501
Stoke-on-Trent	0782-411411

Local Buses

Recent government deregulation has slightly altered bus transport in the region. Some routes saw increased competition, while less 'viable' ones were axed. Some routes are covered by different companies at different times of the day – hence, fares may fluctuate on the same journey. All good monetarist sense.

One characteristic almost peculiar to the West Midlands is the stress that you will cause yourself if you dare to step on a bus with anything but the exact fare. Although it can be quite a good conversation opener with the rest of the bus, it is advisable to have lots of lovely change quietly ripping the lining of your pocket.

Centro oversees all local transport and contracts services out to the companies. Virtually all of the bus routes are covered primarily by **West Midlands Travel** (WMT) or **Midland Red West**. Their hotline, for information on all public transport in the county is on 021-200 2700.

WMT (operators of the classic blue-and-silver vehicles) issue a free and useful (if quite difficult-to-follow) map of their entire network throughout Birmingham and the Black Country, including an essential guide to which stop you need for your chosen bus in the centres of Birmingham, Wolverhampton, Walsall, Solihull and Coventry. Pick up one of these at any travel shop or bus depot, or, if you can't get hold of one and can't fathom out how to get from California to Soho or Londonderry to Maypole (honest!), ring their information line on 021-236 8313.

WMT travel shops will give you all the information, leaflets and toothy smiles that you ever needed at:

Birmingham	114 Colmore Row, 021-200 3334
Dudley	Fisher Street, 0384-53281
Wolverhampton	Cleveland Road, 0902-51601
Oldbury	Halesowen Street, 021-552 7324
West Bromwich	King's Square, 021-525 2555
Solihull	2 Station Road, 021-704 3411

Buses operated by **Midland Red West** cover an extensive network in the conurbation and out to the surrounding towns and villages. Most of the departures from Birmingham city centre go from the **Bull Ring** bus station, which possibly beats even Digbeth coach station (see *Coaches*) for its grim surroundings and depressing atmosphere. It's reached via Station Street or Dudley Street, or using the steps from New Street station forecourt. They also operate limited-stop **Timesaver** buses out to surrounding towns, which are considerably faster than your average 97-horsepower omnibus.

To get to grips with the exciting possibilities that Midland Red offer you, you'll have to cough up 15p for their very comprehensive timetable book. Their only travel shop in the conurbation is in the bowels (almost literally, I'm afraid) of the Bull Ring bus station, although a whole wealth of agencies are detailed in the front of their timetables that can deal with your needs and flog you a ticket or travelpass. A **Midwest Day Rover** (which can also be bought on board your first bus of the day) offers unlimited travel for £3.20 right through the glorious hills, mountains and valleys of Shropshire, Herefordshire and Worcestershire, straying even over the Welsh border. All Midland Red travel enquiries on 0345-212555.

Night Buses

These have been severely cut back in recent years. On Friday and Saturday nights, WMT operate from Colmore Row, Colmore Street and Bull Street (all near Snow Hill station) on the hour, every hour out to fifteen destinations. On the other nights of the week, Midland Red West operate eleven services at 0100 and 0230 from Colmore Row. That's your lot, folks! Ring either company for current prices and details of destinations.

Taxis

Plentiful, but not cheap. At night, the best place to get a black cab in Birmingham city centre is from the rank outside New Street station. These are generally more reliable than mini-cabs, but if you do get a mini-cab (which can work out cheaper), make sure you establish the cost of the journey before getting in the car. Otherwise, you may well find yourself paying the proverbial arm and a leg. Through the nose, no doubt.

The major radio-controlled fleet are the **Taxi Owners Association**, available twenty-four hours on 021-427 8888.

Cycling

Like any metropolis, the West Midlands can be terrifying and dangerous to cycle around during the peak hours of traffic congestion and driver irritability. The *Observer* chose Birmingham's Inner Ring Road as their most daunting cycle track for journalist Sue Arnold. She rightly said that the city was redeveloped in the sixties with the needs of the motorist paramount; her verdict was 'four wheels good, two legs bad, two wheels lethal'.

However, as 'green' consciousness grows, and more people want to take to the roads on their trusty old boneshaker, local councils have made considerable efforts to create new cycle routes (some using canal towpaths). Much of this work was undertaken by the now sadly defunct West Midlands County Council.

Champion of the beleaguered cyclist is the **Birmingham Cycling Project**, and its 'political' wing, **Pushbikes**. As well as making the necessary representations to local authorities and other groups, they publish the invaluable *Cycling Guide to Birmingham*, which covers a good part of the surrounding urban area as well. The guide maps the best routes among the quieter back streets; it also has sections on the law, women and cycling, buying a bike, public transport and bikes – as well as a guide to the green corridors in the city along river and canal banks, and out into the surrounding countryside. Plans are currently afoot with the city council to produce a free guide. Pushbikes will provide legal advice in the event of an accident. Both organizations can be reached at 54/57 Allison Street, Digbeth. The Cycling Project's phone number is 021-631 2916; for Pushbikes ring 021-632 6753. Pushbikes meet every month (currently on the second Thursday) to plan campaigns and strategies of a biking bent.

Cycle hire and sale is not especially well catered for in the area. **Tower Cycles**, run by national record-breaker Alan Richards, sells and hires a vast range of cycles and tandems at 172-178 Gravelly Lane in Erdington (021-373 3679). **Harborne Cycle Surgery** of 16 Wood Lane, Harborne (021-427 6367) hire out tandems and sell ordinary bikes. **On Your Bike!** has recently opened at 10 Priory Queensway (opposite Lewis's) in the city centre (021-627 1590). They sell the cycles and all the hip gear to go with them.

Cars

If you're used to the rush hour London-style, that of Birmingham or any of the towns in the region will seem like a picnic. If, however, you are more used to the traffic in Aberystwyth or Auchtermuchty, the jostle on the Inner Ring Road may come as a heart-trembling shock. Like most conurbations, the traffic congestion has worsened enormously in recent years. In the case of Birmingham city centre, the car throttle of the Inner Ring Road is planned to be scaled down, bringing it down to pedestrian level. Generally, though, it is very easy to direct yourself around the West Midlands. Buy an *A-Z*, follow the signs and go!

NATIONAL TRAVEL

The West Midlands is exceptionally well situated for travel both nationally and across the sparkling oceans. In ascending order of expense and glamour:

Coaches

Birmingham is linked to most of the nation's medium-sized and large towns and cities by the National Express and Scottish Citylink services. Many of these also stop off in Wolverhampton, Stourbridge, Cannock, Walsall and Solihull but your most likely starting point is **Digbeth** coach station in Digbeth High Street, Birmingham B5, just down from the Bull Ring.

Digbeth has carved itself a place in the city's mythology: it is virtually impossible to bounce into Digbeth all carefree and sunny and to sustain it for a tenth of the average delay that you are likely to suffer.

However, Digbeth is a useful getaway point, and, let's face it, your destination can only be an improvement. Coach travel is appreciably cheaper (but slower and often very chaotic too) than rail travel: students and those under twenty-four can purchase a Coach Card (currently at £4.25) giving a one-third reduction on fares. So, it might just be worth braving an hour or three in Digbeth. If you're bored, you can always read the toilet walls....

For all information on coach services, consult your local WMT Travel Shop, or ring Digbeth on 021-622 4373/4225/5371.

Flightlink Royale offer a slightly posher coach to London than your trusty old National Express. Travel in 'luxury and style'. Oh yeah? If you really want to try, contact them on 021-554 5232.

Rail: Inter-City

Birmingham New Street is the hub of the Inter-City network, with many services operating also from **Wolverhampton, Birmingham International** (at the NEC and Airport) and **Sandwell & Dudley**. Thus it's very easy to get to most corners of Britain, which is great news if you're a traveller, if you're trying to persuade friends to come and visit you, or even if you want to slap on your furry-hooded anorak and join the rest of the train-spotting throng on New Street platform 12. Services are considerably better running north-south: trips to East Anglia or Wales can be a bit of an endurance test, as you are likely to get fobbed off with some latterday railway equivalent of the charabanc, euphemistically (and usually wrongly) entitled a 'Sprinter', an 'Express' or 'The Clappers'.

Services to **London Euston** are generally reliable, fast and very regular (every half-hour Monday to Saturday until early evening, and every hour in the evening and on Sundays from New Street and Birmingham International; at least every hour from Wolverhampton and Sandwell & Dudley). The usual quagmire of British Rail pricing means that cheap(er) tickets are strictly rationed to certain trains – from New Street this can mean the difference between £14 and £41 return! It is also pretty easy to get to all other major towns and cities in the country – details of times, destinations and prices can be obtained on the 24-hour enquiries service on 021-643 2711.

AIR TRAVEL

Birmingham International airport, the fifth busiest in the UK and still expanding, is situated at Elmdon, on the A45 Coventry road, next to the National Exhibition Centre. The sparkling new terminal building was opened in the mid-1980s, and reflects the airport's growing stature as a major centre for holiday and business flights. From Elmdon, you can fly to a wide range of European (and the odd North American) destinations, or connect via one of the London airports into the worldwide network.

But, a huge word of warning for non-package flight travellers. It is – in general – massively more expensive to fly that extra hundred miles to Europe from Birmingham than it is to go from Heathrow, Gatwick, Luton or Stansted. For example, it is easy to fly from London to Paris for well under £100. To do the same from Birmingham will generally cost way over £200. In this kind of case, it is probably worth getting the coach from Digbeth to Heathrow or Gatwick (or train to Gatwick from New Street). So much for encouraging the development of the regions – not to mention the noble words being bandied around in Westminster, Strasbourg and Brussels.

Birmingham airport really comes into its own as a package holiday departure point. Many companies and operators fly from here, as you will notice if you have cause to use the airport in July or August, where you will find scores of screaming children, exasperated, sweaty adults and snoring lager boys anxiously awaiting the next 'Cowboy Airways regrets...' call.

Access to the airport by public transport is easiest by the **Maglev** light transit toy train that links it to Birmingham International station. Airport information on 021-767 5511.

Accommodation in Birmingham and the Black Country

LONG-TERM ACCOMMODATION

Despite occasionally resembling a concrete jungle, the West Midlands suffers some dire housing shortages. Council housing is in very short supply and in some disrepair due to a halt on building new property. People come to the area from all over the UK to work, and added to a student population of 30,000, you could be joining thousands of others looking for that elusive decent bedsit or flat in Moseley.

Council Accommodation

All councils in the region use the points scheme, whereby priority cases (e.g. elderly people, those with disabilties etc.) are moved in far ahead of others. If you are not such a priority, and you choose to live in a popular area, you will be waiting an awfully long time. Points are awarded for every year that you spend on the waiting list – indicating that finding council accommodation is not a speedy process. It is impossible to be more specific about how long you are likely to have to wait as this depends on several factors. These include the number of properties available and just how many people are looking for the same kind of housing. In some areas (e.g. Solihull), if you are under twenty-one or have not spent two years in the borough, you will not be entitiled to council housing at all.

Housing Associations and Co-operatives

In the likely event of a long wait for suitable accommodation, there are numerous Housing Associations, two of the largest being **Shape** at 44 Bradford Street, Birmingham 5 (021-622 2747) and **Copec** at 35 Paradise

Circus, B1 (021-631 2525). They are independent, non-profit-making organizations providing fair-rented accommodation for those in need. However, they in turn have their own waiting lists and, in some cases, the council will nominate people already hanging on in there on the points scheme for certain properties.

The major housing co-op organization is **Birmingham Co-op Housing** at 510a Coventry Road, Small Heath (021-773 3583) and 78 Heathfield Road, between Perry Barr and Hockley. Addresses of the many other local housing associations and co-operatives can be obtained from the council.

Hostel accommodation is also available – details of YMCA and YWCA hostels below, although these are just the tip of the iceberg. If you are homeless and have the opportunity to take a place in a hostel, do so, as you will remain technically homeless and thus have a better chance of getting council accommodation.

Private Rented Accommodation

Try to avoid accommodation agencies. Despite the law (Accommodation Agencies Act 1953) stating that no fee can be charged until suitable housing can be found, you can find yourself being charged £30 for an *A-Z* and some rather natty change-of-address cards. If you are looking for anything more than a bedsit, then the fee goes up – merely to have access to the agency's list of properties.

As an alternative, pay a visit to an estate agent dealing with rented property (some councils will provide a list on request). They may not be overjoyed to help without the prospect of a huge fee, but at least it's free. Once you've visited an agent and left your name and address, be persistent and keep phoning until something turns up.

The *Birmingham Evening Mail* (issued at 1130) and the *Wolverhampton Express & Star* carry adverts for all types of rented and private accommodation. If you decide to view a property, arrive early for your appointment as these adverts are always well scrutinized and it's very likely that there are dozens of other hopefuls coming to beam at the landlord in a 'want me' kind of way. Flats and rooms in houses are also advertised in shop windows in the twilight bedsit-world of areas like Edgbaston, Harborne, Moseley and Balsall Heath. However, these areas are also very fashionable, and are especially popular with students from nearby Birmingham University. Therefore, try and avoid searching in September.

Compared with many cities, rents are reasonable. Expect to pay

£15-25 per week for a bedsit or room in a shared house, £30-40 for a flat or more luxurious room. The quantity of rentable places dwindles out of the central areas of Birmingham and Wolverhampton. The bijou suburbs of southern Brum (Edgbaston, Harborne, Selly Oak, Moseley, etc.) are by far the most popular parts of the region to live in, whether renting or shackling yourself to a mortgage.

For help and advice, try your local council's housing department, the nearest **Citizens' Advice Bureau** (look in the phone directory), or the **Shelter Housing Aid Centre** at 191 Corporation Street, Birmingham (021-236 6668).

SHORT-TERM ACCOMMODATION

Hotels and Bed & Breakfasts

The major hotels based in and around the centre of Birmingham are all of a high standard. The NEC and the new ICC have established the city as a prime centre for men in grey suits with expense accounts, as well as acting as an incentive for the building of new hotels. Large luxury hotel chains that have settled in the area include **Hyatt Regency**'s towering ice cube next to the Convention Centre, **Swallow**'s carefully recreated period piece and **Novotel**'s very novo hotel in Broad Street, with another on the way at Birmingham airport. They are all at the far more pricey end of the market (£70-100 per night) but some offer special offers at week-ends to fill the empty beds left by the week-day business bods. Cheaper top-flight hotels can be found in the Black Country: try the **Goldthorn** hotel in Wolverhampton or the **Post House** hotel in Great Barr. Now on to things you can afford...

By far the best way of finding hotel or bed-and-breakfast accommodation at any price from a tenner a night upward is by going through the local **tourist information centre** (for the West Midlands county, see the list at the back of the book, or farther afield, see the *SHIRES OF MIDDLE ENGLAND*). **Birmingham Convention and Visitor Bureau** operate a free accommodation booking service on 021-780 4321. All of the information centres can provide comprehensive leaflets and brochures on the dozens of budget places to hang your hat and call your home.

The best-known organic and wholefood hotel is the small **Ashdale House** at 39 Broad Road, Acocks Green B27 7UX (021-706 3598).

Other Short-term Accommodation

As an alternative to hotels and B&Bs, here are a few interesting places to lay your weary head...

The Birmingham **Youth Hostel** is at Cambrian Halls, Brindley Drive, off Cambridge Street in the city centre (021-233 3044). The **Gorge Environmental Studies Centre** at 83 Gorge Road, Sedgley has accommodation for eight tents or twenty campers, offering field studies and local history courses among other activities. The **YMCA** at 300 Reservoir Road, Erdington (£51 full board for one week) offers canoeing, water-skiing and orienteering, as well as a gymnasium, TV and games room. Details on 021-373 1937. Other YMCAs are at 38 Carters Green in West Bromwich (021-553 4211) and 200 Bunbury Road in Northfield (021-475 6218). Snow Hill YMCA in Birmingham has now closed.

Corresponding hostels operated by the **YWCA** are at 1 Stone Road, Edgbaston (021-440 5345), Penn Road in Wolverhampton (0902-24596) and 76 Alcester Road in Moseley (021-449 3748). Don't despair, by the way, if you are neither 'young' nor 'Christian': the doors of these hostels are open to all ages and denominations.

For the earthier among you, a **camping and caravanning park** can be found at Kingsbury Water Park, Bodymore Heath, B76 0DY, just south of Tamworth (0827-874101), which is open from April through to October and is set in 600 acres of landscaped park, complete with lakes and fairly minimal facilties. For a marginally more luxurious stay, the site at Chapel Lane, Wythall (off the A435 south of Birmingham) is a little more up to date, with wonders of modern science like toilets. It's on a five-acre pitch which is handy as a touring base for south of the city. Details on 0564-26483.

There is little short-term **self-catering** accommodation on offer (the West Midlands not having yet, surprisingly, made it into the timeshare league). However, if you are looking for somewhere to stay during the university/polytechnic holidays, some of the colleges offer lodgings to non-students. Aston University (021-523 6907) rent self-catering properties in Handsworth Wood for not much over twenty quid a week. Wolverhampton Polytechnic (0902-321000) do likewise at Randall Lions House for £30 per week, or £6 per night. Student halls of residence can provide central and convenient accommodation facilities, although it would be hard to pretend that the beds would command a star rating on anybody's scale. Wolves Poly also offers possible accommodation for groups of up to 40 people during term-time in rooms in Dudley and Wolverhampton. In desperation, bed and (soggy) breakfast is available at one of Birmingham University's halls on campus; but at twenty quid a night, the question of value for money should surely be posed. If that's your level of desperation, contact them on 021-454 6022.

2. ROOTS

This chapter is designed to give you the chance to step back from an endless whirl of information and telephone numbers in order to gain a broader outlook on the region and the things that go on within it.

ROOTS covers the towns, cities and villages that make up the West Midlands conurbation, with a bit about their history, feel, politics and media.

Cities, Towns and Villages of the West Midlands

The districts of the West Midlands are rarely viewed as possessing any degree of autonomy: outsiders in particular tend to regard them as one large, sprawling, coal-blackened, funny-accented lump. Do not fall into this trap! The most obvious division to make is between Greater Birmingham (Brum council itself, including Sutton Coldfield and Solihull) to the east of the conurbation, and the Black Country to the west. Even these labels are rather too sweeping and need slightly closer examination.

'GREATER BIRMINGHAM'

The area covered by the two borough councils of Birmingham and Solihull is eclectic in the extreme. At the northern and southern tips lie Sutton Coldfield and Solihull respectively, two rock-solid, very well-heeled Conservative strongholds where a Brummie accent is about as common as it is in Inverness. Sutton Coldfield still deeply resents its loss of municipal status and its incorporation into Birmingham City Council. Both are full of tree- and Jaguar-lined avenues, bursting with minor (and not so minor) managers and directors of firms 'in town'. There's hardly a tree or lamp-post left without a Neighbourhood Watch plaque welded to it.

Between the two lies a huge variety of suburbs and districts, once a distinctive collection of individual towns and villages. Very noticeable is how relatively plush suburbs (such as Hall Green or Edgbaston) nestle rather coyly and uneasily slap next to far less salubrious parts (such as

Sparkhill or Balsall Heath). To the immediate north of the city centre lie some of the older (largely late-nineteenth- and early-twentieth-century) suburbs such as **Aston**, **Handsworth** and **Lozells**, which all became somewhat run down in the post-war years and are now experiencing some flushes of gentrification. The same process can be seen in an exaggerated fashion in the older southern suburbs: **Moseley**, **Ladywood**, **Balsall Heath** and **Sparkhill**. Having passed through the stages of sixties and seventies bedsit-land, property is now being bought up to be spruced up by hordes of pine-stripping first-time buyers.

The south-west of the city is characterized by spacious and graceful districts such as **Edgbaston**, **Harborne**, **Bournville** and **Selly Park**. Despite the fact that many of the map's green spaces have now been assiduously filled in with the stipple of housing, these suburbs have not generally lost their allure to those slightly better-off folk who want to be nearer the city centre than many of their financial superiors in Solihull or Sutton. It is in these southern suburbs that much of the city's gentler and more cultural pursuits take place.

Beyond the inner northern suburbs lies a bewildering array of post-war estates, swamping old villages such as **Great Barr** and **Hamstead**. These pale into insignificance, however, next to the mushroom of suburbs in the extreme east of the city: the mass of high-rise blocks slapped on to Castle Bromwich airfield and given the ironically rural name of **Castle Vale**. 'Lower' versions of similar post-war 'villages' abound here: **Chelmsley Wood** and **Shard End** being among the most evident.

Moving back towards the centre, the east-central side of the city was one of poor suburbs, very heavy industry, vast, rotting, railway yards and rancid canals. Areas such as **Vauxhall**, **Bordesley**, **Washwood Heath** and **Saltley** gradually slipped into a cumulative decay that produced a ghettoizing effect for low-paid workers (often those from ethnic groups), and ensured that the area remained underfunded and under-supported. The area's close proximity to the city centre, however, always meant that one day 'the big plan' would arrive. It surely did, in the guise of the **Heartlands** project, which is intended to bring the high disposable incomes into bijou little pads fronting the limpid waters of the, er, Birmingham & Fazeley Canal. See section on *Heartlands* in *JOY RIDES*.

THE BLACK COUNTRY

What was once deemed an almost unusable epithet for an

area has been turned around into being a proud statement of individuality and spirit. The name of the Black Country has been enthusiastically dusted down to promote the area comprising the four borough councils of Sandwell, Wolverhampton, Dudley and Walsall. They are by no means, however, a homogeneous blob.

The real heart of the Black Country is more hotly contested than is the heart of most teen pin-ups. It could safely be said that it is somewhere in the near vicinity of **Dudley** – probably a little to the north-east of the town. Each town in this area – **Bilston**, **Darlaston**, **Wednesbury**, **Willenhall, Tipton** and **Oldbury** – grew up as self-contained Industrial Revolution-fuelled furnaces revolving mainly around one particular staple industry. Towns and villages a few miles apart would concentrate exclusively and obstinately on one very tiny manufacturing output – perhaps nails, needles, locks, springs or buttons. The area was chronicled as being black and sooty by day, red and fiery by night. The aptly named Black Country was desolate, loveless, hard and, above all, just plain grim.

To the north of the conurbation, the large town of **Wolverhampton** always fared a little better, having historical roots going back to Saxon times, as well as a far greater diversity of trade and industry. In the middle part of this century, Wolverhampton was the kind of town that epitomized all the grind, grit and honesty of the British working class: a thriving manufacturing industry, a religiously followed football team at the peak of the game, and its dog and horse racing tracks. All very decent and stern.

Today, it is a thriving town that has an intimate mixture of cultures and ages populating it. The Polytechnic, right in the heart of the town, brings in students and visitors from all over the world, which many find as a pleasant surprise after the almost automatic sneer that people place in the word 'Wolverhampton', denoting all that is drab and dull. Far from it: if nothing else, you can have one of the best pub crawls in the country here!

The hinterland between what is obviously Birmingham and what most people would classify as the Black Country centres on areas such as **Smethwick** and **Bearwood**: largely industrial, but cheerful and interesting towns that seem to have had some kind of involuntary identity crisis forced upon them. This is the area that is known (in Parliament and the Post Office, at least) as **Warley**, a mystery town that you will not find on any map. To further confuse matters, the area forms part of the unheard-of (and largely unwanted) metropolitan borough of **Sandwell**, which until 1974 was merely the name of a tiny industrial suburb of Smethwick and a large area of parkland. Luckily for the PR men, Sandwell firmly established itself in the 1970s by storming to great and noble victory in the farcical European *It's A Knockout* contest. What a way to establish a town....

The southern and western tips of the Black Country – closer to gasps of the fresh air of Worcestershire and Kinver Edge – were slightly less grimy than their more urban neighbours. **Stourbridge** and **Brierley Hill** produced glass, glass and more glass, as well as housing some of the more wealthy locals – as did Black Country villages like **Amblecote** and **Kingswinford**.

Today's Black Country still bears many of the pock-marks of the industrial acne that afflicted the landscape over centuries. These are gradually being eradicated – both on the vast scale of transforming the old Round Oak steel works into the Merry Hill wonder-world, and more modest local projects of land reclamation or landscaping.

Kissing Babies: the Politics of the West Midlands

At general election times, the West Midlands is usually thrust blinking into the national spotlight and heralded as the barometer of nationwide electoral opinion. 'If the Conservatives can hold Wolverhampton North-East, then this many seats (expansive sweep of hand towards computerized map) will stay blue,' enthuses Peter Snow or equivalent. The map of the West Mids turns a slight shade of red, and it's a sure sign that Neil'n'Glen can nip out and choose some new curtains for Number Ten.

Certainly, a good handful of the parliamentary seats in the urban region are pretty marginal either way. Furthermore, it is the Midlands that has solidly swung behind the Conservatives to bolster the Thatcher years, especially in the very many constituencies harbouring thousands of lower-middle-class votes that have consistently gone to the Tories – often in hitherto solid Labour seats. It's a very stark left-right swing: the Liberals (and their various successive identities) have not held any seat in the Midlands for decades.

After the 1987 election, out of the 25 seats in the conurbation, Labour hold fourteen (of which eleven have majorities of less than 10,000), while the Conservatives have an equally precarious hold on the remaining eleven; the only two rock-solid seats are the unsurprising Tory bedrocks of Solihull and Sutton Coldfield (seat of ex-Cabinet minister Sir

Norman Fowler). The region has spawned some notorious MPs in recent years: Enoch Powell sat for a Wolverhampton seat until his infamous views banished him to the Ulster Unionists, and Edwina Currie, although holding a seat in Derbyshire, cut her political teeth on municipal Birmingham politics. Current notables – on the blue bench – are Anthony Beaumont-Dark, pipe-smoking independent-minded member for Birmingham Selly Oak; the hangin', floggin' voice of Sir John Stokes, MP for Halesowen, Stourbridge and the Empire; Edgbaston's Dame Jill Knight, proposer of the notorious Section (née Clause) 28 of the 1988 Local Government Act, outlawing the 'promotion of homosexuality' by local authorities; and finally, two frequent Tory 'rebels' – the slightly damp Richard Shepherd (Aldridge & Brownhills) and the fearsomely right-wing Nick Budgen (Wolverhampton SW).

On the Labour side, deputy party leader Roy Hattersley walks a delicate tightrope over the Muslim vote in his Birmingham Sparkbrook constituency, while neighbouring Small Heath MP Denis Howell is perhaps best remembered for his position as Minister for Drought in the 1976 heatwave. Deputy Speaker of the House of Commons Betty Boothroyd is Labour member for West Bromwich West, while another woman MP, Clare Short (Birmingham Ladywood), has become the bogey-person of *The Sun* and its following of free-thinking liberals for her anti-pornography (including 'page three') campaigns and her tireless work for British withdrawal from Ireland. Labour's booming, bearded thespian, Andrew Faulds, sits for the decidedly untheatrical seat of Warley East.

Local government is alive and kicking in the West Midlands, despite the hasty murder of the juvenile county council in 1986. Such power that central government had not eroded by this time was passed to the metropolitan borough councils: Birmingham (the largest council in the UK), Solihull, Wolverhampton, Sandwell, Dudley and Walsall. All the councils are Labour-controlled with the exception of true-blue-rinsed Solihull. However, the West Midlands style of Labour local government is far from the 'loony left' scare stories that appear at suitably sensitive times in the gutter press about councils in London, Liverpool or Manchester. Its general sense of moderation predates the reconstruction of the party nationally. This political temperance is particularly evident in Birmingham City Council, led by a rare bird indeed, a Labour knight, Sir Richard Knowles.

Birmingham City Council has been at the forefront in trying to push the city to unheralded heights of international fame, bringing considerable criticism from all quarters in the city to the effect that this has been done at the expense of the local poll-tax payers themselves. The council really does seem to have its municipal fingers in a multifarious range of pies, with its V-shaped logo appearing in the unlikeliest of places. The council is a tight ship, a bastion of the 'old school' of local government where officers and councillors close rank against the hostilities of the outside world. Such hostilities have included the years-old controversy surrounding severe malpractice and abuse in some council children's homes, which no-one yet seems to have to answer for. Another example is the council's role in the massive redevelopment work currently going on: they are enthusiastically bulldozing or gentrifying whole swathes of the city, sometimes with callous indifference to the protests. Unusually for a socialist administration, they are a minority shareholder in the private Heartlands project. On a more immediate level, the city council recently took the progressive step of sacking a straight teacher who raised the topic of homosexuality in a sex-education class. *The Sun* is hardly likely to come down heavily on this Labour council.

Despite its tendency towards old-fashioned authoritarianism, the city council has instigated many exciting and innovative projects that seem like a genuine (if occasionally misplaced) attempt to serve the million-plus inhabitants of this huge area. Especially notable are the many arts and cultural events that this administration has spawned in recent years, bringing the city into a hitherto unknown spotlight of national and even international attention.

The other Labour-held metropolitan authorities (Sandwell, Dudley, Walsall and Wolverhampton) are as politically restrained as their large neighbour. They have all come together in an orchestrated attempt to push themselves as one big Black Country industrial heritage park.

The Local Press and Media

NEWSPAPERS AND MAGAZINES

Two of the nation's largest regional daily newspapers spring from the West Midlands: Birmingham's *Evening Mail* and – bigger still – Wolverhampton's *Express and Star*. The *Evening Mail* is part of the Ingersoll group, along with its morning sister the *Birmingham Post* and their Sunday sibling the *Sunday Mercury*. The *Post* and *Mail* provide a solid enough local news service, although sticking to a tried-and-tested formula that has remained unchanged for years. Their combined position is one of sheer brute strength, rarely deigning to dip a dainty toe in the murky waters of Midlands mega-bucks or council complacency. Recent competition has left the *Post* in its most exposed state for many years – probably even since its launch 130 years ago. The *Express and Star* is the brash, bright upstart, now cheekily poaching readers from the *Post* and *Mail* patch well out of its native Black Country. It was the nation's first high-tech paper, converted early to colour, and has consistently made the running in recent years as the all-important 'voice of the region'. The *Mercury* is the West Midlands' only Sunday paper, which is reflected in its status as a rather 'homely' and low-key Sunday supplement – very few readers buy this as their sole Sunday paper.

The *Birmingham Daily News* is another challenge to the old *Post* and *Mail* squirearchy. The nation's first free daily, the *News* was launched by the ever-expanding Reed International group in 1984, and is delivered to over 275,000 homes daily. They have a very deliberate strategy of targeting the ABC1s – pompous socio-economic jargon for the professional classes. Thus, many parts of the city (Harborne, Selly Oak, Solihull and Sutton Coldfield for example) receive absolute saturation coverage, while in those nasty old areas such as Handsworth, Small Heath, Bordesley, Rubery and Sparkhill, penetration can be as low as three per cent of households. Their stated 'positive policy of community involvement' still has a way to go, therefore.

The West Midlands suffers greatly from the lack of a decent regular listings/arts magazine. Towns and cities far smaller than Birmingham and the Black Country manage to sustain innovative and informative publications. But nothing here. To confuse matters, there are two magazines (and different permutations of each one) imaginatively called *What's On*. Neither is particularly interesting: both cover very mainstream events and places and have little editorial. Currently, the only other magazine is *City X*, formerly *City Unlimited*. There is little predictability with *City X*: fine, if that extended only to the writing and the ideas, but a little hard to grasp if that same unpredictability permeates its entire ethos, its politics, its date of arrival in the shops, where to find it, its cover price (or not, as the case may be) – or, indeed, whether it has yet gone under.

Other magazines include *Focus*, a freebie that makes *What's On* look like *Time Out*, and *Warwickshire & Worcestershire Life* (which covers the whole West Midlands too), although this is most definitely the green-wellie Stratford and Malvern side of the region. The West Midlands is bursting ripe for a decent listings/arts magazine – someone hear this plea!

Arts and **music** papers include the notable freebies *Brum Beat* and *Jazz in the Midlands* (see music sections in *THE TWILIGHT ZONE*). West Midlands Arts produce an excellent creative writing journal called *People to People*. Contributions to West Midlands Arts, 82 Granville Street, Birmingham B1 2LH.

RADIO

For years from the mid-1970s, the West Midlands settled into a cosy pattern of local radio listening. A handful tuned into the essentially earnest but dreary **BBC Radio Birmingham**; a far larger and more reckless crowd worshipped Brum-based independent **BRMB**, while **Beacon 303** ruled the Black Country from its Wolverhampton stable. The contest was an eternal stalemate.

The first change was made by the Pebble Mill moguls to zap up the BBC station and to give it a funky new name – er, **Radio WM** (FM: 95.6 MHz, MW: 1458/828 kHz). But people evidently fall for this kind of thing, since the station's ratings slowly started to rise out of the morass and give BRMB some real competition. In fairness, WM's new name wasn't the only major improvement as the station started to take on some more innovative programming ideas. Among their stars now are ex-Tiswas (happy days!) front-man Gordon Astley and the 'campaigning' (if sometimes a little bombastic) Ed Doolan. In these days of split frequencies, WM has hived off its 1458 kHz medium-wave slot to **Heartlands** radio – not the in-house lift music for the development area so named, but a genuine East Birmingham community-based 'neighbourhood' station broadcasting from Saltley. (Well, it sounds better than Radio Saltley....)

Not to be outdone, **BRMB** (FM: 96.4 MHz) also spawned a new creature in its own image, catchily entitled in an eighties kinda way, **Xtra-AM** (MW: 1152/1359 kHz). A joint venture with Coventry's Mercia Sound, Xtra aims to provide 'classic hit radio for Warwickshire and the West Midlands'. Star of the station is true Midland legend **Les Ross**, currently on the weekday breakfast show. It was his informal, often risqué style and humour that have been so widely copied by many Radio One DJs. Catch the original.

As if WM and BRMB doing self-reproducing amoeba impressions wasn't enough, Beacon also went in for a quickie self-divorce. The main station moved on to the FM wavelength (on 97.2 MHz), while the medium wave 990 kHz went to **WABC**, which may sound rough and contemporary (and, most importantly, American), but which in fact stands for Wolverhampton and the Black Country. WABC warbles jingles at you explaining that it is 'nice'n'easy radio' – the aural equivalent of pine air-freshener.

The real boat-rocker came in mid-1990 with the launch of a new Birmingham independent station, **Buzz FM** (FM: 102.4 MHz). Here they operate minimal DJ intervention, ultra high-tech equipment with impressively silly names, their own news-gathering and relay system and a claim to 'serve the soul, the mind and the feet'. Pretentious, *moi*? It could be unkindly said to represent designer yuppie radio, as the target audience is most definitely not Doris from Erdington – more like Rupert from his carphone on the M6. Not that they do phone-ins anyway – heaven forbid! The music is not generally chart-based, but a blend of soul, jazz and funk. Buzz is a brave innovation, and – from their appropriately swish setting in the Jewellery Quarter – they represent a vote of significant confidence in Birmingham as a 'seriously happening' city.

TELEVISION

Regional TV in the Midlands consists of the ancient duopoly of the **BBC Pebble Mill** operation and the decade-old **Central TV**. For most people, Pebble Mill represents rather wistfully remembered wishy-washy lunchtime institutions such as *Pebble Mill at One* and its successor *Daytime Live*, evoking memories of days off school lying under a tartan rug on the sofa and wanly taking in the potted plants, MOR music, chirpy recipes and toothpaste-commercial-type presenters. In actuality, BBC in the Midlands has produced hundreds of other nationally networked TV and radio programmes, including major dramas, provocative documentaries and excellent comedy. Not forgetting *The Archers*. Their regional programming is thorough, if largely unremarkable: despite *Midlands Today*'s array of awards for regional news production, the pitfalls of this sort of TV are as evident here as anywhere. It's a cosy, chatty sort of set-up that rarely threatens, campaigns or enthuses.

As in most places, the independent station has a slightly brasher, more upbeat image than its BBC rival. Central took over the Midlands franchise from Lew Grade's ATV. Part of the deal was that they gave the semi-new station more Midlands perspective – beyond merely giving it a Midlandy sort of name. As one of the largest ITV companies, Central inevitably contributes copious amounts of programming to the national network. Notable among its stable – apart from the ex-*Crossroads*, of course – are *Blockbusters* and *Spitting Image*. Local programming is a mite more exciting than that of the BBC, although the regional news service is much the same standard. Central have commissioned slightly bolder regional work, including Mentorn's youth-styled what's on programme *First Night*, a veritable wealth of information thrown at the viewer with the characteristic belief that 'yoof' have the attention span of a bored goldfish. There is also a **video box** in their HQ in Broad Street, Birmingham to record your lambaste for Channel 4's *Right to Reply*.

Beyond the terrestrial TV stations, satellite dishes of all shapes and sizes are springing up on many a house frontage, as are various cable companies, including the **021 Birmingham Cable Corporation**, which hopes to be broadcasting from mid-1991.

MEDIA PLACES AND EVENTS

In 1985, the **Birmingham International Film & TV Festival** was inaugurated as a rather contrived attempt to cash in on the contemporary desire to throw a couple of vaguely related events together and call it a festival. This one, however, taking place every September, is now recognized as one of the best in the UK. Debates, premières, special screenings and guest stars are now commonplace during the festival.

Birmingham's developing importance as a media centre was reflected by the setting up in 1989 of the **Media Development Agency** to co-ordinate and promote the multifarious organizations and activities that concerned themselves with people in spotty bow-ties. They are based in Digbeth, the area of the city that developers have designated as the Media Quarter in the 'Great Brum Plan'. Pity everyone else is in the Jewellery Quarter....

Wolverhampton's **Lighthouse Media Centre** is an open resource for those who want to see a film or exhibition, attend a workshop or get involved with the media training that is on offer. You can find them next to the Art Gallery, just off Lichfield Street (0902-312033).

3. MILK AND HONEY

Where to Eat in the West Midlands

Not so very many years ago, there were but a handful of places in the region where you could go in and sit down for a decent meal. Such places as there were charged amounts way beyond most people's pockets. Only a couple of decades later, the variety and sheer amount of eating places must surely be enough for anyone – especially in the foreign food categories.

'RESTAURANTS OF NOTE'

For the more discerning (and plump-walleted) diner, there is a new hallmark of gastronomic excellence operating in the region: the catchily titled Proprietors' Association of Trading Restaurants of Note, which, in a tortuously contrived way, produces the acronym **PATRON**. They should perhaps be called the Proprietors' Restaurants for Ingesting Classy, Irresistible Edibles – or PRICE. A guide to these chosen 22 restaurants is available from Tourist Information Centres. Some of them (La Galleria, Franzi's, Chung Ying Garden, Maharaja, Jonathan's) are mentioned in other sections, several others are hotel restaurants. Most large hotels have high-class restaurants: of particular note are the **Castillane** at the Midland Hotel (English cuisine using local produce); the **Terrace** at the Birmingham Metropole (NEC) and the **Belfry** (French food plus the rather savoury hors d'oeuvre of 370 acres of parkland and golf course).

EUROPEAN FOOD

Traditional **English** (yes, we *are* in Europe) food is no more easy to find here than it is in just about any other city in the country. Probably the most well known restaurant is the Victorian **Jonathan's** at 16-24 Wolverhampton Road, Bearwood (021-429 3757), which can only really be afforded on very special occasions. Even if you can't afford to eat, just have a good salivate over the wine list. For the continental taste, start at **Le Provencal** at 1 Albany Road in Harborne (021-426 2444), a family-run restaurant providing fine **French** food and some hearty vins. **Chez Julien** at 1036 Stratford Road, Shirley (021-744 7232) is recommended for its fresh produce, much of which is imported directly from France. Flame-grilled Welsh lamb, however, is a speciality. **Sloans** in Chad Square, Edgbaston (021-455 6697) serves immaculately cooked and presented, over-priced nouvelle cuisine. **Michelle Restaurant Français/La Santé**, which shouldn't tax anyone's 'O' level French too hard, is a cosy and reasonable place at 182 Harborne High Street (021-426 4133). Cheaper still, and worth investigation, is **Silverside Grill** at 27 Warstone Lane in Hockley (021-233 3655). **Spanish** cuisine with a particular bent for seafood can be found in an unlikely setting next to the Inner Ring Road at the **Casa Paco** at 4 Fletcher's Walk (021-233 1533), behind Birmingham Central Library. **Los Canarios** goes in for those Costa del classics like paella and calamares – at 105 Albert Street in the heart of Brum (021-236 3495).

The area is often said to lack many very good **Italian** restaurants, although there should be enough to satisfy most folks. Two very renowned (and not especially cheap) ones are **Giovanni's** (doesn't sound quite so special as 'John's Cafe') in Poplar Road, King's Heath (021-443 2391), and **Giuseppe's** at 36 Hill Walk, Northfield (021-475 6233). **La Galleria**, in Paradise Place in the city centre (021-236 1006), manages to combine a fairly authentic Italian atmosphere with meeting the demand for semi-fast food for corpulent businessmen at lunch-time. It's also quite reasonably priced. At the other side of the city centre, at 3 Park Street, off Digbeth, is **Lorenzo's** (021-643 0541), which is atmospheric, serves excellent food but is not too cheap. In Chad Square, Edgbaston, **Ristorante Pinocchio** (021-454 8672) will help something a little further down from your nose grow to vast proportions with an excellent menu and good atmosphere. **Valentinos** at 73 High Street, Harborne (021-427 2560) is quite pricey, but very tasty.

Very much cheaper, but filling and vaguely Italian, is **Pastificio** at 102 New Street, central Brum (021-643 1548). **Pepito** at 36 School Street in Wolverhampton (0902-23403) is a hearty, cheap and very cheerful Italian filler. Needless to say, everywhere – especially in Birmingham city centre – there are endless pizza chains.

Franzl's Austrian restaurant at 151 Milcote Road, Bearwood has PATRON's seal of much-coveted approval for its genuine Austrian chef. Book on 021-429 7920. The more famous Austrian cuisine is the cream-laden fancies that we associate with Strauss waltzes and Viennese coffee houses. Although the West Midlands may not conjure up such images, **Druckers Viennese Patisserie** in the graceful Piccadilly Arcade off New Street in central Birmingham comes close to creating that elegant and old-fashioned sophistication and gluttony. There are also branches in the Great Western Arcade and the High Street in the city centre, Sparkhill, Moseley, West Bromwich, Solihull and Dudley Street, Wolverhampton.

The best **Greek** eatery in town is **Bambos** at 61 Station Street (021-643 5621), which can get pretty lively at times, but which serves excellent food. For the classic mix of Greek food and some pissed lad from Saltley trying to belly dance, head on to the indomitable **Salamis** at 178 Broad Street (021-643 2997) on the edge of the city centre in Five Ways. In some of the suburbs there are various other notable places, including the originally named **Acropolis** taverna at 608 Bristol Road in Selly Oak (021-471 4696).

For food and drink in the **Jewellery Quarter**, see *JOY RIDES*.

ASIAN FOOD

One of the greatest surprises in the West Midlands is the Pakistani **Balti** dishes that are served in so many restaurants only in this region. If you are a curry fanatic, you will certainly get hooked on Baltis, which are chunky stews of meat, fish or vegetables cooked in a rich and spicy curry sauce in a karahi or round cast-iron dish, and eaten straight out of the dish with nan bread or similar. Many Balti restaurants are absurdly cheap but not licensed to sell alcohol – though you can usually take your own. Frequently, there is an off-licence handily placed next door – often, not surprisingly, owned by a relative of the restaurant owners. As a result of all these idyllic factors, the best Balti houses are very busy.

Some parts of the region abound with Balti houses, resounding to the tune of belches from packs of prowling tanked-up boys lurching from door to door. Sparkhill and Sparkbrook are especially notable for the sheer number of Balti houses on offer.

Yasser Tandoori Restaurant at 1268 Pershore Road in central Stirchley (021-433 3023) provides a good, dirt-cheap, middle range Balti (as well as other dishes) in the almost-clichéd red flock-wallpaper, red light and sitar music atmosphere. Unlicensed – take your own. East African, as well as Asian, food of a mouthwatering standard is available at the **Kilimanjaro** at 9A Walford Road in Sparkhill (021-771 3994). In the principal Balti district you'll find – amongst many others – the **Royal Alfaisal**, at 140 Stoney Lane, Sparkbrook (021-449 5695), which can be thoroughly recommended, if only for its indecently sized nan breads. Stoney Lane and Ladypool Road are the heart of Balti-land, with dozens to choose from. Other worthy Baltis are the **Nirale** and the **Sharma** on Moseley Road, near Bordesley station, the **Kashmiri Cottage** on the

Highgate Road, Sparkbrook, and the **Punjab's Paradise** in Ladypool Road.

Adil Tandoori is the most famous Balti house in the area, having been featured in magazines, newspapers and on TV. Its reputation has somewhat moved beyond its reality, and, although the food can be bettered in other restaurants, it is still very lively and great fun. Unlicensed. 150 Stoney Lane, Balsall Heath B12 (021-449 0335).

Many of the Balti and Indian restaurants open well into the wee small hours. Two neighbouring restaurants at the Five Ways end of Broad Street open extremely late – **Regards to** (179 Broad Street – geddit?!) opens until four o'clock every morning (021-643 4021), and the **Ne-Shah** at No. 180 provides a good cheaper scoff where you can bring your own drink (if you haven't had enough by then).

For the best selection of savouries, sweetmeats, breads and vegetarian snacks, the **Milan Sweet Centre** at either 191 Stoney Lane or 238 Soho Road, Handsworth, is your joint.

The overwhelming number of establishments makes it very difficult to pick out just a few, and of course there are many other Indian restaurants throughout the area. One of the most celebrated (and justly so) is the **Dilshad Tandoori** in Berry Street, Wolverhampton (0902-23481), which also offers live music and a magic show on Thursdays, as well as a doorman in impressive oriental garb. The **Bilash** is another excellent curry house in Wolverhampton, set (appropriately) in Cheapside (0902-27762).

Upmarket Indian restaurants include the **Maharaja**, encroaching on to the borders of Chinatown at 23-25 Hurst Street (021-622 2641), and the **Rajdoot** in Albert Street (021-643 8805). Both are excellent, luxurious, not very cheap and recommended by PATRON for their excellent North Indian cuisine in suitably swanky surroundings. In between these and the cheap Balti houses are the two branches of **J Jay's**, serving good and delicate curries at 1347 Stratford Road in Hall Green (021-777 3185) and in the Edgbaston Shopping Centre (021-455 6871).

Topoli at 1480 Pershore Road in Stirchley (021-459 6867) is the city's best-known **Persian** restaurant. It's reasonable, very tasty, very friendly and you can bring your own wine.

See below for some of the best Indian and Balti restaurants serving decent vegetarian food (although nearly all have some meat-free choices). The ones mentioned below are all good for carnivores too.

VEGETARIAN AND WHOLEFOOD

In these enlightened days, virtually all eateries offer some kind of vegetarian alternative. However, if you are getting a little cheesed off (ahem...) with those baked spuds and half-microwaved veggie lasagnes, take a trip round some of these. Remember that many vegetarian restuarants are unlicensed, so it is often possible to take your own booze.

There are very few veggie-only eateries in Brum city centre, with **Natural Choice** in the Pavilions Food Gallery one of the only options.

One of the best known in the region is **Ginger's Vegetarian Eating House** at 7a King's Heath High Street (021-444 0906). Quite small, it has no-smoking areas and some live music at week-ends. Unfortunately, it is not very cheap and plays on its customers' even karma by serving rather mean portions. **Nutters** at 422 Bearwood Lane, Bearwood (021-420 2528) carries on the age-old tradition of giving a good vegetarian restaurant a stomach-churningly dinky Laura Ashley name. Fully licensed, open lunch and dinner except Monday.

Wild Oats at 5 Raddlebarn Road in Selly Oak (021-471 2459) offers simple food (lots of salad) in plain surroundings, with a daily changing menu and three-course meal for £8 per head. Good for vegans. At 182 Harborne High Street, veggie and vegan food is served at **La Santé** (see above), which, hardly surprisingly, is French, as well as at the **V & A** at the Midland Hotel in New Street, central Brum. The **Amazon Café** at the Friends of the Earth centre at 54 Allison Street, Digbeth, is the place to level your biorhythms with some carrot juice and matching cake. Take your own salt....

If you don't want to drink or smoke, the **Cornerstone Café** at 25 Woodbridge Road in Moseley is run by a Christian charity and serves mostly vegetarian food. The **Healthy Way** at 87a Darlington Street, Wolverhampton, is another small café serving a fair selection. Star of the café section has to be **Zebedees** at 190 Alum Rock Road in Saltley, which serves organic food grown by their own fair hands and sold at ridiculously low prices.

When you tire of trying to find that elusive veggie heaven, pop into any Indian or Balti restaurant for a fine, cheap meal. Vegan food and a take-away service is available at the immensely popular **Rajput Tandoori** in The Square, Codsall (0907-44642), and the **Golden Gate** at 38 Townend Square, Park Street, Walsall provides vegetarian versions of many dishes to be taken away or eaten within earshot of their cabaret accompaniment. Both the **Dilshad** and the **Bilash Tandoori** in

Wolverhampton are recommended for their vegetarian choices. **Omar's** Kashmiri Restaurant at 167 Hagley Road, Edgbaston, have a vegetarian buffet every second Sunday and a great selection at other times – they are unlicensed but you can take your own plonk. **Jaanneman's** is a vegetarian Gujerati café set in the heart of Balti-land at 279 Ladypool Road (021-449 6801). Cheap and bloody marvellous.

CHINESE & THAI

Chinatown in central Brum is the area around Wrottesley Street and Ladywell Walk off Hurst Street. Although it currently resembles a building site, the end result is intended to be a focal point for the region's Chinese culture and cooking. Even now, there are plenty of good restaurants here, including the excellent Cantonese **Chung Ying** in Wrottesley Street (021-622 5669) with the obligatory surly waiters (but fabulous food). Do not confuse with the **Chung Ying Garden**, around the corner, which is nowhere near as good.

Other worthwhile pig-out places in Chinatown are the **Satay House** at 69 Hurst Street (021-622 1313), which serves barbeque-style Chinese food and is good for the veggies; the **Forbidden City** at 36 Hurst Street (021-622 2454), which houses a large casino upstairs and serves dim sum from 1200-1800, and a full menu until midnight; the eminently reasonable **New Happy Gathering** at 43 Station Street (021-643 5247). Also coming soon is the Chinese riposte to McDonalds, a fast-foodery with a menu pared down to twenty of the most popular dishes.

Out of the city centre, try the **Rainbow** (021-444 4195) at 59 King's Heath High Street. The best thing about the famous **Shirley Temple** in Stratford Road, Shirley (021-744 1855) is its name – but, sadly, that won't fill you up. **Henry Wong's**, at 283 Harborne High Street (021-427 9799) is the superior elder sibling to **Henry's** in St. Paul's Square.

Thai food is growing in popularity, as it combines some of the subtlety of Chinese food with the flavour of Indian. With huge dollops of peanut sauce. The best – if quite expensive – Thai restaurant in town is the **Thai Paradise** in Paradise Square (021-643 5523). Also highly recommended – and a little cheaper – is **Pranees** at 816 Bristol Road, Selly Oak (021-471 5029).

THE AMERICAS

The ominous advance of the burger bars has somewhat clouded our vision of **North American** food. Sure, much of it does consist of big burgers cooked and dressed in ever more fanciful ways, although there are plenty of other things to pick from. Vegetarians do tend to get fobbed off with some mega-salad. **Rock Candy Mountain** at 176 Harborne High Street (021-426 2481) produces good-value good food. **TGI Fridays** at 180 Hagley Road in Edgbaston (021-454 1930) provides substantial, reasonably priced but hardly exciting food, as does **Jeffersons**, at 563 Hagley Road West in Quinton (021-422 2515), which advertises itself as a 'concept' restaurant capturing the 'richness and the hospitality of the deep South of America'. Those for whom this sort of thing strikes a resonant chord of anticipation might also be inclined to stampede along to **Branegans Rib and Rack Bar** at 192 Broad Street (021-643 5100).

For a **South American** tang on your taste-buds, try the hugely popular, remarkably cheap and very atmospheric **Los Andes** at 806 Bristol Road in Selly Oak (021-471 3577).

In between the two is **Mexico**, whose food is now one of the most popular for any night out. There are few such restaurants around, the best probably being **Cisco's** (021-359 2283) at 45 Curzon Street, just to the east of the city centre. It's not cheap – especially the drinks – although it's got a good, lively atmosphere.

CAFFS, SANDWICHES AND SNACKS AND CAFÉ-BARS

The good old **greasy spoon** is far from dead in the region. The perfect hangover cure is a plate of neat cholesterol, on offer on virtually any of the major routes radiating throughout the West Mids.

Lunchtime **sandwich bars** abound in the area around the flash district of St. Paul's Square. These are definitely not of the limp Mother's Pride with a transparent sliver of cheese variety. The **Upper Crust** in Caroline Street and the nearby **La Baguette** are both particularly delicious.

Birmingham city centre has a moderate selection of cafés. All the major department stores (including **Lewis's** and **Rackhams**) have good restaurants to soothe the weary shopper, as do the shopping centres. The saving grace of the **Pavilions** shopping centre is a multi-choice restaurant on the top floor which is especially good for the indecisive. You could always try the **Virgin Megastore** café for an overpriced baked spud in chrome surroundings. The best and the most tranquil of the cafés are in the museums and galleries around the region: the café in **Birmingham Art Gallery** is a riot of genteel Edwardian splendour and is unmissable. The **Triangle** at Aston, **MAC** in Cannon Hill Park and **Wolverhampton Art Gallery** all have small, but atmospheric, cafés. **Druckers** are a series of hugely indulgent Austrian coffee shops – see *European Food.*

Following the runaway success of the bar at the **Repertory Theatre** in Broad Street, the other theatres have leapt in on the act. The **Alexandra** has opened **Gershwin's**, which desperately tries to be oh-so-chic, and **Thorpe's Brasserie** has opened at the **Hippodrome**, Hurst Street.

For a good old yuppie lunch, don the stripy shirt and head for **Hawkins Café-Bar** at 205-219 Corporation Street. The place gets packed in the evenings with neighbouring Aston University students.

If none of the above tickles your palate, how about guinea pig? Not eating one, but being one – at the **College of Food & Domestic Arts** in Summer Row, central Brum, where the eager young chefs of tomorrow try out their creations on you in their restaurant. Ring for details on 021-235 2774. See *JOY RIDES* for more details.

Brum and Black Country Pubs

Birmingham and, especially, the Black Country have been renowned for their ale since the mid-nineteenth century. It is not difficult to see why. Some of the stonking bitters and milds of the region should convert any erstwhile lager-drinker. Not *all* the pubs are the kind of vast 1930s M&B monstrosity that you come across on just about every roundabout in suburbia – take the time to venture a little more off the beaten track and you should find that the voyage of discovery is a happy one....

THE SMALL BREWERIES OF THE BLACK COUNTRY

Many Campaign for Real Ale enthusiasts would cite this largely unknown part of the country as their Mecca. Small, fiercely independent breweries still survive alongside genuine pubs that combine hospitality, solid food, excellent beer and enjoyment without a trace of a neon light or too much overplayed re-created Victoriana.

Batham's is one of the most well-known and well-established small brewers, based on Delph Road in Brierley Hill (see *The Canals* in *JOY RIDES*). Fronting the brewery is their excellent flagship pub, the **Vine** (unofficially the Bull and Bladder). They have seven other pubs – four in and around Kidderminster and Kinver, three in the Black Country: the

Royal Exchange in Enville Street, Stourbridge, the excellent **Lamp Tavern** (notable for its mouthwatering collection of malt whiskies as well as the beer) in Dudley Lower High Street and the **Holly Bush** in Bell Street, Pensnett. Tours of the **Batham's Eight** were once commonplace, although these are now viewed with suspicion bordering on hostility by some of the landlords and regulars, thanks to some of the 'macho' behaviour that such excitement raises in weak minds. However, a tour taking in the pubs is certainly worth investigating – the brewery will supply information, and can be contacted at Delph Road, Brierley Hill DY5 2TN (0384-77229).

Holden's of George Street, Woodsetton, Dudley (0902-880051) is a long-established family brewery that can be toured on Saturdays. They have around twenty tied pubs, including the brewery frontispiece, the **Park Inn** on George Street, Woodsetton. In Wolverhampton, the superb **Great Western** is one of Holden's best known pubs. You can find it in Sun Street, at the back of Wolverhampton station. The **Trumpet** in Bilston High Street (buses 225/6, 262, 334, 401, 525/6/7, 530, 545/6) goes for a potent and occasionally sweaty (but always excellent) mix of Holden's and nightly (lunchtime on Sundays) live jazz. Definitely worth the journey. At 106 Franchise Street (off B4200 Park Lane between Wednesbury and Darlaston) lies the **Cottage Spring**, a popular and thoroughly enjoyable Holden's backstreet local. Bus 327 passes the door. Farther south, in Heath Lane, Stourbridge, the **Shrubbery Cottage** serves a fine pint of Holden's to sip as you make a complete prat of yourself on its bowling green.

Holt, Plant and Deakin display cheery red signs at their twenty-odd houses throughout the Black Country. Although a part of the monolithic Allied Breweries (and thus slightly overplaying it on the 'cutesy semi-independent' image), the end result is a very fine pint indeed. The **Holt's Brewery** pub on Station Road, Langley Green, Oldbury (almost next to Langley Green station or buses 120, 441/9) is where Entire and Deakin's Downfall are brewed – the mild and bitter are unromantically trucked down from Cheshire. You can sit in one of the vast pub rooms, chomping your beef and gravy or black pudding doorstep sandwich, and gaze lovingly into the innards of the brewery, tours of which are operated by Black Country Tours. Details on 0384-231751.

Other notable and eminently visitable Holt's hostelries include: the Black Country Society's fortress, the **Church Tavern** in Quarry Bank High Street near the Merry Hill Centre; the **Fountain Inn** in Owen Street, Tipton town centre, just down from the station – complete with mementoes of the area's renowned nineteenth-century boxer, the 'Tipton Slasher'; the excellent **Swan** in Lower Street, Tettenhall; the **Posada** in Lichfield Street in central Wolverhampton – possibly the best pub in the town centre, beautifully tiled and with a genuinely relaxed and original feel. Wolverhampton's answer to the Rover's Return.

The **Old Swan (Ma Pardoe's)**, on the Halesowen Road in Netherton (0384-253075) – buses 243/7/8, 283, serves its own home-brewed delight. Ma Pardoe herself died only a few years ago, but there is no chance of her pub disappearing too – it has, in fact, recently been extended into nearby premises. The pub is a Real Ale shrine, as it has been around a great deal longer than the current fad for beers of the ilk of Polkington's Old Scrote. This is not a carefully recreated Real Ale nook – the beer, the food, the enamel tiling and the atmosphere really have changed little over decades. An absolute must.

The other side of Dudley sees the **Beacon Hotel** in Bilston Street, Sedgley (0902-883380), where the renowned **Sarah Hughes Original Mild** is brewed in the restored tower brewery behind the hotel. Sarah Hughes ran the pub and brewed her own from 1921 through until 1958. Her grandson decided that the brew was too good to lose, and reopened the brewery in 1987. The Mild is a dark and pretty strong beer that dashes any sneering asides that a pint of mild is akin to drinking the slops. Buses 256, 545/6, 558 – and, believe me, you'd better get the bus.

A recent newcomer to the scene in the Black Country and Worcestershire is 'Mad' O'Rourke's **Little Pub Company**. One thing is certain – Colum O'Rourke is far from mad, as he has watched his early couple of houses blossom into many of near-cult status, attracting visitors from miles around. His recipe is easy to understand: slightly zany pubs built around improbable themes, serving quasi home-brewed beer (Lumphammer ale), huge pies and other excellent food.

The **Little Dry Dock** on Windmill End, Netherton (see *The Canals* in *JOY RIDES*) has a narrowboat as its bar; there is the aptly named **Pie Factory**, just off Hurst Lane and Sedgley Road in the centre of Tipton (buses 226, 545); the **Cradley Sausage Works**, just up from Cradley station on the High Street (buses 127, 136/7, 232, 242/3); the **Little White Lion** with its gaudy mock stained glass, on the A458 Stourbridge Road in Halesowen (buses 9, 247/8). Each pub – and the ones out in Bewdley (the **Pack Horse**), Kidderminster (the **Little Tumbling Sailor**), Alcester (the **Lark**) and Worcester (the **Sauce Factory**) – present an array of quirky and often very funny themes and ideas, including a wry in-house newspaper and a passport to all the pubs. The **Little Pub Company** – its 'Unspoilt by Breweries' motto mocking that of Banks's – is on the verge of expanding nationally from its intrinsically local base. Shame, really.

THE TITANIC BREWERIES

Into the big boys' league right across the region, we reach the **Wolverhampton and Dudley Breweries**, which sub-divide into the Siamese twins of the Midlands breweries, **Banks's** and **Hansons**, joined at the taste buds. Serving nearly one thousand pubs throughout the Midlands, the beers are good standard drinks – Banks's Mild being a particularly worthwhile surprise.

Davenports, based in central Brum, is a recent victim of a huge takeover by the ruthless north-western firm of Greenall Whitley. Nonetheless, the finished product is still very much a firmly local brew that – when kept well – is quite delicious. **Ansells** lost its virgin independence back in the sixties as a founder-member of the gigantic Allied Breweries. A good pint of Ansells is not at all uncommon, although it is rarely something that will make you want to jig naked down the High Street.

Mitchells and Butlers, or M&B, are the archetypes of the huge, fizzy keg beers in the region and part of the vast Bass group. Their **Highgate Mild**, however, is still brewed at the old brewery in Walsall and it is a great drink. The huge M&B brewery at Cape Hill, Smethwick, can be visited. Details on 021-558 1481.

OTHER NOTABLE BLACK COUNTRY PUBS

Although the Real Ale meccas tend also to be the best pubs in the area, there are a good few other excellent taverns worth investigating. In an area that takes the pub so seriously, you're never very far from one. One of the great bonuses is that the Black Country is among the cheapest drinking areas in Britain.

Brierley Hill has a good deal more to its drinking notoriety than merely the Batham's headquarters and ready-made pub crawl along Delph Road (see *The Canals* in *JOY RIDES*). The **Bull's Head** in Bull Street (off Brettell Lane) is an excellent Banks's pub that regularly hosts live bands. On Merry Hill, sitting rather uneasily in the growing shadow of the fast-spreading shopping centre, lies the Ansells pub, the **Robin Hood**, with its **Citizens' Theatre**, home of the original, the best and the bawdiest **Black Country Night Out**. Details on 0384-77756. Farther up the road towards Dudley is the lesser-known, but certainly worthwhile, art-deco **Woodside** in Woodside Road.

Dudley town centre has some other fine pubs that are worthy of an hour or two of pleasant quaffing: the **Old Vic** in King Street offers an ever-changing selection of guest beers in a slightly garish setting; the snug, very unpretentious and unspoilt **Shakespeare** in Stafford Street is well worth a couple of hours serious supping. Salop Street, on the way out to Gornalwood, contains two fine pubs: the genuine and very friendly **British Oak**, serving the semi-home-brewed Skittain Ales and occasional ciders, as well as a healthy dose of occasional jazz, and the **Struggling Man**, an old farmhouse that is the epitome of a traditional Black Country pub. Dudley also hosts an annual **Real Ale Festival** every Spring Bank Holiday, giving you the ideal chance to lose yourself, your wallet, your self-respect and your bladder control – all in one weekend!

Continuing on the B4176 Himley Road to Gornalwood, as the edge of the town is reached there is a small track to the left that takes you down to the **Crooked House** (officially the Glynne Arms), one of the most famous Black Country pubs, though hardly for its beer. Set in a cross between a moonscape of old workings and a rural enclave, it is built on land that has subsided and sent the structure of the pub in all kinds of bizarre directions, which can be pretty disorientating even before the first sip.

Into the heart of the Black Country and to some fabulous, unsung pubs, well away from any possible tourist trail. Just north of Dudley town centre is the town of **Tipton**, home of the Fountain Inn and the notorious Pie Factory (see above). In Lower Church Lane (B4163) near Dudley Port station is the **Old Court House**, a very bare, very traditional, very boozy and very male stronghold that is nevertheless worth a visit. Between Dudley and Oldbury, in the district of **Tividale** is the stonking **Barley Mow** pub on City Road, off the A4123 New Birmingham Road. There are some really excellent views over the Black Country from this pub, set high up on Darby's Hill. Also has good food and a skittle alley.

In **Wednesbury**, apart from the already mentioned Cottage Spring, there is a converted 400-year-old coaching inn with the rather forcedly ancient name of **Ye Olde Leathern Bottel** in Vicarage Road. On the road to **West Bromwich** at Hill Top there is the solidly traditional **Sow and Pigs**, notable for its murals. Farther on into West Brom town centre, the **Old Hop Pole**, in the High Street, is a reconstructed traditional Holt's Black Country local, pork and gravy sandwiches and all.

The **Oldbury** and **Blackheath** area contains the Holt's brewery (see above), as well as some very worthwhile old pubs. In Church Street, central Oldbury (near Sandwell & Dudley station) is the **Waggon &**

Horses, serving many different brews in an original tiled and shining copper setting. In the same street is the excellent and – to use a much-quoted word – 'cosy' **White Swan**. In the Blackheath/Old Hill borders, make the effort to discover the musical Holt's pub, the **Beech Tree Inn** on Gorsty Hill Road; just around the corner towards Old Hill station in Station Road is the exalted canalside **Wharf**, offering great beers and some very good food. Off Station Road is Waterfall Lane, home of the amenable and deservedly popular **Waterfall**.

Slightly to the west is the area of **Cradley Heath**. Lurking in an industrial estate behind the High Street is the superb (but not very originally named) **Swan**, serving a well-kept pint of Holden's on the corner of Providence Street and Foxoak Street. On Reddall Hill Road, farther up Cradley High Street, is the lively and very Black Country **Waggon & Horses**.

At the extreme south-west of the conurbation, **Stourbridge** has a couple of notable pubs within the compact town centre – apart from the Shrubbery Cottage and the Royal Exchange (see above), there is the hugely popular **Old Crispin Inn** in Church Street, which gets packed mainly due to its excellent food and young atmosphere. The **Duke William** in Coventry Street provides a very civilized respite from the shopping centre, as does the **Seven Stars** in Brook Road, Oldswinford, serving some far better than average pub food. A mile to the west of the town centre is the suburb of **Wollaston**: visit the **Foresters Arms** or the **Unicorn** on the A458 Bridgnorth Road or the wonderful and very friendly Davenports hostelry, the **Bull's Head** on Wollaston High Street. On the A458 Stourbridge Road in **Halesowen** the commonly named **Waggon & Horses** has an uncommonly large selection of ales in a very welcoming environment. **Lye**, to the east of Stourbridge, has the excellent and genial **Shovel Inn** on the A4036 Pedmore Road.

The area around **Wolverhampton** contains many rewards for the intent drinker. The town centre offers an excellent venue for a thoroughly amnesia-inducing pub crawl – apart from the Posada and the Great Western, mentioned above, some of the greater watering holes include the modest-looking **Combermere Arms** in Chapel Ash (the road Darlington Street becomes after the ring road); the **Lord Raglan** on Great Brick Kiln Street, just off St. Mark's ringway, where the food is diverse and excellent, catering well for vegans and vegetarians; the theatrical **Sir Tatton Sykes** opposite the Grand in Lichfield Street. The **Barley Mow** in Stafford Street is a regular venue for live music and comedy.

Neighbouring **Bilston** boasts some fine ale-houses: the jazz pub, the

Trumpet (Holden's – see above) in the High Street, where you'll also find the fifteenth-century converted manor house, the **Greyhound and Punchbowl**, complete with resident ghost that supposedly walks around the pub with a glass of whisky, and is largely to be seen in the Ladies! One too many pints of Highgate Mild? The **George and Dragon** (otherwise known as the **Clog**) down the A463 at 104 Broad Lanes (take the Coseley Road from the High Street) is a real local that has a superb atmosphere. The **White Rose** opposite Bilston Town Hall on Lichfield Street is another Highgate pub where the beer is very well kept.

The **Walsall** district is not so well known for its ale, despite the locally brewed M&B **Highgate Mild**. In Butts Street, opposite the Arboretum, is the Ansells local the **Butts Tavern**, a regular venue for live music. Just outside the town centre, the studenty **White Lion** in Sandwell Street becomes very lively at times. Another student haunt, with regular live music, is the nearby **Wheatsheaf** on Birmingham Road. In the town centre, the **Duke of Wellington** in Birmingham Street is a popular and old-fashioned pub that serves an excellent Highgate Mild. The **Green Dragon** in the High Street is another goody. Off the A34 Stafford Street in John Street is the **New Inn**, otherwise known as the **Pretty Bricks**. Good food and very popular. The **Punch and Judy** at 40 Walsall High Street has a regualar late (well, midnight) disco on Thursdays.

INNER BIRMINGHAM

The city centre and surrounding districts are full of pubs – some of them have the atmosphere of an old sock and are well worth avoiding. However, there are still plenty left in which to spend those few pennies.

The **city centre** suffers from a lack of evening 'locals', simply because no-one really lives there. The pubs and wine bars are therefore geared towards lunchtime or early evening trade, or simply as Friday and Saturday night stepping-stones in which to pour endless lagers down willing throats before the stampede to the local night clubs. Evidently popular is the **Slug and Lettuce** in Thorp Street, where the music is so loud it's a good idea to go there only with people you really don't want to talk to. The smell of rising libido and overwhelming after-shave makes any Friday night here a rare experience for the nostrils. At the end of Thorp Street, on the Horse Fair, is the theatrical Davenports hostelry, the **White Lion**, that is usually an entertaining start to the evening. A little bit farther down, in Wrentham Street off Bristol Street is the old Irish local, the **Fountain**, easily worth the ten-minute stroll from the city centre.

Atkinson's bar, in the very plush Midland Hotel, Stephenson Street, is a surprisingly easy place to enjoy (if a little pricey). They offer a fine selection of beers in a comfortable setting, slightly reminiscent of a posh library. In another nearby hotel – the **Midland** in New Street – the **V&A Bar** is a fairly good shot at sophistication shaken but not stirred. At the other end of the spectrum, in Lancaster Circus, in the pleasant setting of the ring road flyover, the **Turk's Head** is great if you want to eat, but rather a disaster if you want to have a drink with it.

Henry's, at the top of Hill Street opposite the Town Hall, is an attempt at designer paradise: paradise, of course, is a very subjective concept. On the other side of the racing track laughably known as the Inner Ring Road is Gough Street and the very popular **Gough Arms**, which takes considerable pride in its vast selection of beers.

Near Five Ways station and the Accident Hospital is the small and very friendly **Bull's Head** in Bishopsgate Street – worthy of a stroll if the spruced-up hostelries around the nearby International Convention Centre get too much. Try also the **Unspoilt by Progress** in the utterly spoilt by development Five Ways Shopping Centre. Farther along the Hagley Road is the enduringly popular **Ivy Bush**. The pubs in the vicinity of Broad Street and the International Convention Centre have been ruthlessly tarted up to accommodate hordes of grey suits from the world over. One of the grand old Victorian inner-city pubs, M&B's the **Crown** has suddenly found itself slap next to the ICC. As a result, it is clean, bland and too expensive. Next door is the **Brasshouse**, which also appears to be trying to shoot itself upmarket, especially with its **Celebrity Restaurant**. Almost opposite, in Gas Street, is the seriously superior cocktail/wine bar **Arthur's**. Tucked away in a bit of a back alley, it never seems very full, although the décor and clientele are agreeable enough. Quite good (though pricey) food is available – just enough for those who overindulge to chuck up later in the toilets of neighbouring **Bobby Brown's The Club**. For other pubs around Gas Street and the canals of the city centre, see *JOY RIDES*.

The **Jewellery Quarter** and the area around **St. Paul's Square** contain a fair few taverns, although most have been dolled up to the nines to reflect the area's new found-kitsch status. Details are in the section on *The 'Quarters' of Birmingham* in *JOY RIDES*.

The best central area for backstreet locals, music pubs and some good old-fashioned crawls is to the south-east of the city centre, around the **central markets, Digbeth, Deritend** and **Highgate**. The district contains lots of small street-corner establishments that often look pretty grotty from the outside, but which conceal unpretentious, friendly interiors. A quick run through some of them: the **Spotted Dog**, at 21 Bordesley Street, a compact and lively pub that frequently has Irish bands playing and a quiz at the week-end; the **Market Tavern** in Moseley Street, Digbeth, another frequent live-music venue serving excellent lunchtime food for the market traders and shoppers; on Deritend High Street Birmingham's oldest pub – going back to the thirteenth century – the half-timbered **Old Crown**, frequently playing host to folk nights; the **Carpenter's Arms** in Alcester Street and the **Pig and Whistle** in Barford Street – both solid locals, with a surprisingly upmarket clientele; the **Lamp** in Barfort Street, with one of the best ranges of beers in the city; the **Cannonball**, in the romantic setting of the gas works in Adderley Street, one of the city's leading jazz establishments (see *THE TWILIGHT ZONE*); the **Little Bull** in Digbeth, which serves the best Irish beer in town; the games-orientated local the **Woodman**, opposite the old Curzon Street station. Then, the surprise of them all, **Moby Dick's** in Penn Street (off Curzon Street), an amazing find in such an out-of-the-way location: the nautical theme extends throughout, right to the excellent and rather offbeat seafood restaurant upstairs. Book on 021-359 5923. In nearby Jenners Road, the **Black Horse** is a music pub that puts on live bands and indie discos. Highgate's Gooch Street contains the ever popular **British Oak**. Near Bordesley station is the quirky and prized **Brewer & Baker** in Ravenshurst Street. The **Forge** in Fazeley Street has weekend discos and many live bands.

The inner suburbs to the north of the city centre contain some excellent places to fritter away your hard-earned cash. The **King of the Road** in Hospital Street, off New John Street West in **Newtown**, is particularly notable for its excellent food at lunchtime. **Aston** not only has the Villa, it also has the **Barton's Arms** on the corner of High Street and Park Lane – a vast Victorian pile that is very near to being The Ultimate Pub. Faded elegance, chipped dignity and a sumptuous interior just aren't enough, it seems, for, as this book goes to print, one of the city's finest pubs is due to be closed by M&B breweries. It will be a crying shame should it happen.

Off the Lichfield Road, near Aston station, is the small but perfectly formed **Manor Tavern**. In towards the city centre, and cowering in the shadow of the Inner Ring Road, are two popular establishments: the cosy **Gunmaker's Arms** in Bath Street and an Ansells Heritage pub, the **Bull's Head** in Loveday Street. Nearby, next to Aston University, is the hugely popular and often rowdy **Sacks of Potatoes** in Lister Street and an occasional music venue, the **Pot of Beer** in Holte Street.

Over the other side of Spaghetti Junction is the excellent and ancient coaching inn, the **Lad in the Lane**, in Bromford Lane, **Erdington**. Farther round the A4040 Outer Ring Road to the west is the unglamorous but comfortable **Hare & Hounds** in Marsh Hill.

Perry Barr has some good local pubs that warrant a few leisurely evenings. The **New Crown and Cushion** on Birchfield Road looks a little grotty on the outside, but the far more important inside is brilliant. The **Wellhead Tavern**, behind Brum Poly in Franchise Street, serves great food and a good choice of beers. It has recently been named Birmingham Campaign for Real Ale's Pub of the Year. A little farther west is the **Grove Hotel** in Oxhill Road, Handsworth, which has a superb atmosphere, as well as laying on some excellent live music.

OUTER BIRMINGHAM

One of the most reputed areas for pubbing is that around **Moseley**, **Selly Oak** and **Balsall Heath**, especially as these are still largely student and young people's districts. Moseley's most famous pubs are the **Fighting Cocks** in St. Mary's Row and the **Trafalgar** in Woodbridge Road: popular, rowdy and very busy – especially as preparation for a night's serious dancing. On the Alcester Road, the **Prince of Wales** is a further very popular, pretty relaxed, studenty pub. Another of the big and popular breed of pubs is the **Hare & Hounds** in nearby King's Heath High Street, with occasional live cabaret and even the odd male stripper! In the same street is the excellent **Station**, a cosmopolitan if slightly tweedy place that puts on a good range of dance and live music, as well as a Tuesday night women-only bar and disco. The **Eagle** at 189 Mary Street, Balsall Heath, is a great example of true Brum hospitality.

In Stirchley, the **Lifford Curve** on Fordhouse Lane is one of the best of local pubs, with some pretty average competition. The Banks's and Hanson's are particularly well kept. The **Three Horseshoes** on the Pershore Road in central Stirchley gets pretty lively at the weekend, and is definitely worth a try if you're feeling sociable. A little farther south, in **King's Norton**, is the sturdy Davenports' local, the **Navigation**, set next to the Worcester & Birmingham Canal on Wharf Road. The **Breedon Bar** at 1652 Pershore Road, Cotteridge is an well-known and imaginative place that hosts very many good live bands.

To the east of the city centre are the posh bits of **Harborne** and **Edgbaston**, as well as the not so posh bits of **Smethwick** and **Bearwood**. In central Harborne – 'the village', don't you know – you can find some suitably charming and chic little establishments, including the **King's Arms** in the High Street (hosting regular **folk nights** on Tuesdays), and the **White Horse**, around the corner in York Street. The **Bell** in Old Church Road is a peaceful if rather hoity-toity ex-coaching inn.

Just off the A457 Dudley Road in Smethwick is the remarkable **Bellefield** in Winson Street. It's an old home-brew pub, with many of the original and unusual features and decorations intact in its various rooms. More incredible original interior design can be seen in the **Waterloo** in Smethwick's Shireland Road, where the stunning old tiling helps to bolster the excellent and unpretentious atmosphere.

Apart from the multi-use **Bear Tavern** (cabaret and live music) in Bearwood Road (see *THE TWILIGHT ZONE*), Bearwood also has another regular music venue in the **King's Head**, on the corner of the main A456 Hagley Road and Lordswood Road.

The eastern outer suburbs are the land of the squat, modern pub that is largely functional, but rarely exciting. There are a few exceptions, especially in the older areas such as **Stechford**, where the converted **Cole Hall Farm** on Cole Hall Lane stands out as being a little different.

4. JOY RIDES: DAYS OUT AND ABOUT

Musemums and Galleries

THE 'BIG' ONES

Birmingham Museum and Art Gallery

- **Location:** Chamberlain Square, city centre; 021-235 2834. Any bus to city centre or train to New Street or Snow Hill.
- **Times and cost:** Open Mon-Sat 0930-1700, Sunday 1400-1700. Free.
- **Disabled access:** Wheelchairs to some galleries; better to phone.
- **Children:** No facilities.
- **Facilities:** Café/restaurant serving excellent food.

The Pride of the City lies at the back of the council chambers in the staunchly Victorian municipal Chamberlain Square. The permanent exhibition is excellent, and houses many notable artists of all periods and styles. Reputedly, the most impressive Pre-Raphaelite collection in the world is here. Special exhibitions are nearly always on, frequently with some local relevance. Recent examples have included a fascinating look at Midlands photography, a superb Pissarro exhibition, satirical prints and drawings and work from the local silver and jewellery industry.

Undoubtedly, this is one of the most relaxing and enjoyable few hours that you can spend in the city centre. Don't miss the amazing period Georgian tearoom with its vastly impressive black-and-white tiled floor, serving twee teas as well as more substantial fare. You can often sip your Darjeeling to the strains of a live chamber quartet or a pianist.

Birmingham Museum of Science and Industry

- **Location:** Newhall Street, city centre. Any bus to city centre or trains to New Street or Snow Hill; 021-236 1022.
- **Times and cost:** Mon-Sat 0930-1700, Sunday 1400-1700. Free.
- **Disabled access:** Wheelchair access good.

- **Children:** Great for toddlers upwards, no crèche.
- **Facilities:** Shop and 'coffee area' (Maxpax machine and Formica tables).

Cowering under Birmingham's rather pale and ugly imitation of the Post Office Tower lies a very enjoyable way of spending a blustery afternoon. The region's industrial past is laid out before you in hulking pieces of machinery, photographs, locomotives, pistons and engines. You don't really need to be a boffin to appreciate it, although some of it is quite technical. Most importantly for kids of all ages, there are plenty of buttons, handles and knobs to press, turn and twiddle. If you can dodge the screaming school parties and weary Joyce Grenfellesque teachers, you can indulge your experimental fantasies in the 'hands-on gallery', the Light of Science. Those far-off days of school science were never like this... .

Black Country Museum

- **Location:** Tipton Road, Dudley; 021-557 9643. BR Tipton station 3/4 mile away or buses: 226, 245, 262, 310, 311, 312.
- **Times and cost:** Daily 1000-1800. Admission £3.75 adults (+£1.50 for canal trip). Reduced prices for children and pensioners.
- **Disabled access:** Wheelchair access good to the site.
- **Children:** Victorian funfair and baby-changing facilities.
- **Facilities:** Pub, café and tea room.

One of the most successful museums in the country and winner of many heritage and tourism awards, the museum is the spearhead of the Black Country's bid to be taken seriously as a marketable area – successful despite the sneers of just a few years ago.

The large site is littered with uprooted Black Country buildings and artefacts that the visitor can wander around at random – a tram, a cottage tilting through mining subsidence, an engine house and others. In one cluster is the museum 'village', an uprooted collection of authentic old shops, cottages, workshops and the Nonconformist chapel slap next door to the 'Bottle and Glass', a superb old pub that serves a very fine pint of local brew indeed.

A new exhibit is the underground trip through a mine, 'Into the Thick'. Here, you are transported around fibreglass coal-faces in the company of the taped voice of one Lija Wedge, later encountered in glorious plastic persona. Nonetheless, it's a very effective way of beginning to appreciate the conditions under which men, boys and horses worked. At times you are bent almost double getting down a narrow, dark and low passage to the tune of water drips, coal falls and the recreated smell of dankness and sweat.

For a further £1.50, you can take a barge into the depths of the 200-year-old Dudley canal tunnel, which plummets for two miles under Castle Hill and the town centre. The trip takes you to the 'Singing Cavern', a natural limestone quarry in the bowels of the hill, where the visitor is now exposed to a high-tech state-of-the-art 'multi-media experience', telling the story of the canal and the tunnel. It probably is worth the extra money, although it's advisable to buy your separate ticket on arrival at the main entrance of the museum – you could otherwise have to wait for hours. Longer trips are available – details from Dudley Tunnel Trips Ltd, Unit 44, High Street, Tipton DY4 8HH (021-520 5321).

A good deal of just criticism is aimed at some of our tourist 'Heritage' industry. The Black Country Museum succeeds where many others fail (for starters, very many visitors are local) in educating in a proud, not patronizing way. A very interesting – if far from cheap – day out.

Cadbury World

- **Location:** Bournville, Birmingham B30 2LU; 021-433 4334. Trains from New Street to Bournville (Redditch line), adjacent to the factory and museum. Buses 24, 27, 80, 227, 280.
- **Times and cost:** Mon-Sat 1000-1730, Sunday 1200-1800. Adults £3.75, children £2.75.
- **Disabled access:** Yes, except for the factory gallery.
- **Children:** Play area for toddlers, baby-changing facilities.
- **Facilities:** Shop, self-service restaurant.

Serious chocoholics beware! The ultimate theme attraction opened in summer 1990 to provide an insight into a family firm that has left an indelible mark on Birmingham's life and history. Cadbury were always more than just another city factory – they pioneered worker participation and spacious, hygienic work and living conditions in an era when being a trade unionist was a deportable offence (how history repeats itself...), culminating in the Cadbury brothers building the revolutionarily well-laid-out suburb of Bournville for their workers. The museum looks at their history, as well as that of the brown, gooey stuff with which they made their fortunes. In approximately an hour and a half you will learn hosts of hitherto unknown things about the good old choccy bar: for instance, Did You Know that some ancient tribes in Central America worshipped Gods of Chocolate? If you add the deities of Gin and Valium, you can see we've turned a full circle.

Wolverhampton Art Gallery

- **Location:** Lichfield Street, WV1 1DU; 0902-312032. Five minutes from railway and bus stations.
- **Times and cost:** Mon-Sat 1000-1800. Free.
- **Disabled access:** Ramped entry, helpful staff, toilets.
- **Children:** Education service, nothing for toddlers.
- **Facilities:** Tea room – with deee-licious cakes!

A quiet, spacious gallery in the heart of Wolverhampton, this is well worth an hour or two of browsing time. Exhibitions are particularly unusual and innovative, although the permanent collection covers a stunningly wide range too. Fossil-lovers should head for the new Frazer Gallery, while the Wolverhampton Room hosts a great exhibit of the town's links with the metal industry.

Walsall Leather Centre

- **Location:** 54-57 Wisemore (Littleton Street), WS2 8EQ; 0922-721153. Buses and trains to Walsall town centre.
- **Times and cost:** Tues-Sat 1000-1700 (Nov-March 1000-1600); Sunday 1200-1700. Open Bank Holiday Mondays. Free.
- **Disabled access:** Wheelchair accessible.
- **Children:** Special events throughout the year.
- **Facilities:** Coffee shop, leather goods and souvenir shop.

Not the great sex emporium of the West Midlands, but another heritage industrial museum celebrating a town's waning staple industry. The Leather Centre opened in 1988 to show the world what a thriving hub of industry Walsall was, building footballs, shoes, jugs, bellows, musical instruments, clothes and bottles – and all from wonderfully versatile animals' parts.

SMALLER GALLERIES AND MUSEUMS

Art and Culture

The **Barber Institute Of Fine Arts**, on Edgbaston Park Road at Birmingham University's East Gate, maintains its slightly aloof position from 'public' galleries by strenuously declaring its status as part of the University. To all intents and purposes, however, it is 'normally open to individual members of the public during the hours it is open to members of the University'. These are 1000-1700 Monday-Friday and 1000-1300 Saturday. The collection is maintained with this same kind of gentle decorum and taste, and includes work by many notable artists – including Manet, Magritte, van Gogh, Corot, Degas, Gainsborough, Rubens, Turner, Toulouse-Lautrec and Gauguin. Well worth a detour – accessible via University station or any bus down the Bristol Road (021-472 0962).

Birmingham city centre's **Ikon Gallery** is the area's leading proponent of new and experimental visual arts. Many artists from all over the world display in an impressive diversity of exhibitions. The gallery also has a shop stocking those essential arty reproductions for your wall, and a rather natty little coffee shop. It's at 58-72 John Bright Street (behind New Street station and the Pallasades) B1 1BN, 021-643 0708. The Ikon is free and open from 1000-1800 Tuesday until Saturday (2000 on Thursdays). Wheelchair access is good to all galleries.

Regular exhibitions are mounted in various parts of the Birmingham **Central Library** in Chamberlain Square (021-235 4511). Even if that wasn't the case, the Library is full of some fascinating stuff: the world's biggest Shakespeare collection (apart, of course, for one in the good ole US of A), a brilliant Local Studies department, a quirky shop and mile upon mile of groaning bookshelves.

On the other side of the city centre lies the multi-purpose **Triangle Arts Centre**, containing an interesting photography gallery. Details in *THE TWILIGHT ZONE*. **Poseurs**, in Ladypool Road, Balsall Heath (021-442 4543) becomes a venue for some of the city's festival events, as well as a regular gallery for the arts, especially photography.

Walsall Museum and Art Gallery contains the usual municipal collection, but also a couple of startling secrets that surprise any casual visitor. Most notable is the **Garman Ryan Collection** of fine art, donated in 1974 by the widow of sculptor Sir Jacob Epstein. Apart from works by Epstein himself, the collection includes a dazzling array by artists such as Matisse, Renoir, Picasso, van Gogh, Monet, Cézanne, Degas, Turner,

Gauguin and Rodin. A step way above your average council pride and joy. The museum also contains the **E. M. Flint Gallery**, which hosts many varied touring exhibitions. All this comes for free on Monday to Friday from 1000-1800 and on Saturdays from 1000-1645. The museum is above Walsall Central Library in Lichfield Street (0922-653135). Wheelchair access to the galleries.

On a far more intimate level is **Helios Gallery** at 25 Valentine Road (just off the High Street), Kings Heath, B14 7AN (WMT buses 35, 50 or Midland Red buses 177/8/9, 27, 69). A friendly, bustling private gallery in a large Victorian house that exhibits and sells local and other artists' work at all price levels. They also sell home-made mirrors and offer a framing service. Wheelchair access is not great, but help is readily available (021-444 1585). Another excellent and very contemporary gallery with good local content is **Connections Arts** in Rocky Lane, Aston (021-333 3212). **Jubilee**, at 84 West Bromwich High Street (021-553 6862), goes in for a good deal of art and culture from local groups and individuals, a lot of which is excellent. **The Cave** is a multi-arts and community centre at 516 Moseley Road, Balsall Heath (021-440 0288), that acts as a great focus for a good deal of Black arts in the city.

HISTORICAL HOUSES AND HERITAGE MUSEUMS

Perhaps the best known is **Aston Hall and Park** (WMT buses 11 – the Outer Circle route – or 7 from the City Centre, Midland Red buses 110 or 116 from Edgbaston Street or the train to either Aston or Witton stations on the Walsall or Lichfield lines). Pride of the city, Aston Hall is conveniently situated next to a motorway, as all great Jacobean country houses should be. It is open daily Easter-October 1400-1700, and costs nothing to see. However, you won't see anything if you're in a wheelchair or stilettos. More details of this highly desirable property on 021-327 0062.

Similarly historic, on Blakesley Road in Yardley you will find the 400-year-old **Blakesley Hall** (WMT buses 11, 15, 17, 59, 69, 90, 96/7, or a mile long stroll down Station Road from Stechford railway station). An Elizabethan farmhouse in an area not generally thought of as the natural haunt of Young Farmers, the hall has identical opening times and policies to Aston. No wheelchair access; details on 021-783 2193. A short stroll away across the A4040 (Stoney Lane/Station Road) lies **Yardley Village** – not a perfume theme park, but a collection of beautifully preserved buildings (including the ancient parish church of St. Edburgha, a smithy and some almshouses) that serves to remind you how all these rather interchangeable suburbs were once quiet Warwickshire villages.

Like Aston and Blakesley, **Sarehole Mill** is administered by the city council, with the same opening times and rules of entry. It is an eighteenth-century water-powered mill, which (as long as the lake is full enough) still has the wheels in full operation. Located on Cole Bank Road in Hall Green, it is reached via a short walk from Hall Green BR station or from WMT buses 4, 5, 6, 11, 41, 53 or Midland Red bus X20. Details on 021-777 6612.

Willenhall's **Lock Museum** is just that, as well as proof that there is a town somewhere that had lock-making as its staple industry. And this is it. A charge of around £1 for adults lets you step back in time – yet again – to the Victorian era to watch suitably clad demonstrators display their skills. It's at 54, New Road in central Willenhall (buses 325/6/7, 333, 341, 525/6/6A/7/9, 966) and open Monday-Saturday 1000-1700. No facilities for people in wheelchairs.

If locks aren't enough to put a zing in your day, how about glass? Yep, glass. The **Broadfield House Glass Museum** in Compton Drive, Barnett Lane in Kingswinford, near Stourbridge, capital of the glass industry. The museum is free, and examines the history of glass-making from the Roman period until today, using studios, audio-visual displays and some demonstrators. Open Tuesday-Friday and Sunday 1400-1700, Saturday 1000-1300 and 1400-1700. Many of the local glass companies are open to the public, offering tours and seconds shops. Details from the local Tourist Information Centre.

The Oak House in Oak Road, West Bromwich, is another example of a Tudor residence nestling surprisingly in a West Midland town. This one comes complete with a rare Lantern Tower, period oak furniture and fine gardens. Buses 401 and 404 pass very close, and West Brom bus station is only a ten-minute walk away. Free admission. Open April-September: Monday-Wednesday and Friday/Saturday 1000-2000, Thursday 1000-1300, Sunday 1430-2000; October-March: Monday-Wednesday and Friday/Saturday 1000-1600, Thursday 1000-1300. No access for wheelchairs.

The **Jerome. K. Jerome Birthplace Museum** in Walsall is worth seeing if you're within a few streets of it anyway. A small collection of artefacts commemorate the author best known for the wry tale of 'Three Men in a Boat'. Free entry, Monday-Friday 0830-1700, Saturday 0830-1600. The museum is in Belsize House, Bradford Street, minutes from the rail and bus stations (0922-653135).

TRANSPORT MUSEUMS

Birmingham Railway Museum at Tyseley (next to Tyseley station on the A41 Warwick Road: buses 36/7, 44) hosts an impressive selection of railway memorablila (anoraks, thermos flasks, Tupperware boxes etc. – only kidding!) for spotters of all shapes, ages and sizes. You can also hire a saloon coach for parties or eat in 'Chuffs' (oh dear!) restaurant. Small entrance fee, open daily 1000-1700 or dusk (021-707 4696).

Birchills Canal Museum in Old Birchills (off B4210 Green Lane) in Walsall, was opened in summer 1990, at the foot of the Walsall locks. Open Tuesday-Thursday and weekends 1200-1500. Admission free (0922-645778).

The **National Motorcycle Museum** is out on the Coventry Road at Bickenhill, just beyond Birmingham airport at the junction with the M42. If hundreds of motorbikes – and British ones at that – are your thing, this is Nirvana. Also has restaurant and souvenir shop (021-704 2784).

The **Patrick Collection Autoworld** demonstrates the affection heaped on the automobile over the past century or so. Set in a Victorian paper mill, and in the elysian charm of a semi-rural and canal-side setting, Autoworld has been painstakingly built up to represent one of the foremost private collections in existence. Games, radio-controlled cars, beautiful gardens, excellent restaurant. 180 Lifford Lane, Kings Norton (021-459 9111). Buses 11, 45, 47, 145/6/7/8, 166, X6, or a ten-minute walk from either Bournville or King's Norton BR stations. Open mid-May-end of October daily (except Tuesday) 1030-1730 (weekends and bank holidays 1000-1700).

OTHERS

The **Museum of Catering** at the Birmingham College of Food and Domestic Arts is an unexpected treat in the heart of the city (on Summer Row, by the Paradise Circus roundabout on the ring road). Culinary delights, recipe books, kitchen implements, styles and fashions are shown throughout the ages in this small museum. Some implements more closely resemble medieval tortures or sex toys. Here too, of course, is the fabulous college **restaurant**, which allows all the young, creative caterers to try their wares on the public. You may be surprised by what you eat, but you surely won't be disappointed. Details of the museum and the restaurant (both open during college term times) on 021-235 2774.

More Offbeat Days Out and About

THE CANALS

It is a commonly – and truthfully – stated boast that Birmingham has more miles of canal than Venice. As you cross the city, and head into the Black Country, you continually glimpse stretches of canal in varying degrees of regeneration or putrefaction. All of the councils in the area have been making a great effort to reopen miles of the network, once again available as a serious method of transportation for both business and pleasure. Miles of oil-slicked ditch are being gradually teased back into green slices through an often grey city.

The major canals in **Birmingham** converge on the prosaically named **Gas Street Basin**, which, until very recently, was a decrepit, genteel enclave in the heart of a fume-filled city. It was a real surprise – and delight – to stumble across. Nothing, it seems, lasts for ever, and once the planners and brown-sign erectors had discovered it, Gas Street was incorporated into the mass gentrification/development plans for the Broad Street/International Convention Centre area. The derelict warehouses were rebuilt as executive marina flats and a Beefeater restaurant/hotel, imaginatively named the **Wharf**. The determined upmarketing continued apace with the development of the Mitchells & Butlers showpiece waterfront pub the **James Brindley**. When it opened in 1986, the erstwhile residents and regulars of the Basin barricaded the bar with oil drums as a protest at the growing incursion and threat to their lifestyle. Since then the tarting-up process has continued at breakneck pace: the **International Convention Centre** and the towering glass of the new **Hyatt Regency Hotel** now dominate the Basin, struggling to hang on to its last scraps of virgin mystery. But for how long?

Epitomizing this change are two long-established canal-carrying companies still just about hanging on in there in the Basin. **Second City Cruises** (021-643 4384) and **Parties Afloat** (021-643 0525) are run by people for whom the canals and the Basin are a way of life. They acknowledge that they probably have little time left in the Basin in which to operate, as they suspect the city council has plans to relocate them in order to make the Basin more easily fit its shiny new coat. Services include camping trips on water, parties, very reasonably priced one- or two-week holidays as well as regular scheduled trips for part of a day or the evening to some local places and pubs. **Brummagem Boats**, around the corner in Sherborne Street Wharf (021-455 6163), are much larger and more upmarket (and less interesting) than their two near neighbours, and thus more integral to the visions of the city council. They offer similar routes.

The **canal-side walks** from Gas Street are fascinating: wildlife, animals and rampant nature conquering old industrial units, while, in turn, being systematically upstaged and uprooted by mushrooming new development. A very interesting walk is to head north under Broad Street from Gas Street Basin, right past the canal front of the ICC and up to **Brewers' Basin**, the junction of three canals, a couple of hundred yards away. The right-hand fork is the Birmingham & Fazeley (near Tamworth) canal, taking you down towards Cambrian Wharf and the Science Museum, through a flight of locks and the notable canalside Ansells pub, the **Long Boat**. This route has provided the first *Canal Walkway Guide* leaflet, produced by the Birmingham Inner City Partnership.

The left fork at Brewers' Basin is the beginning of the 'motorway canal', the Birmingham New Main Line, built by Thomas Telford to cut straight through to Wolverhampton, replacing its winding, contour-following predecessor, not surprisingly called the Old Main Line. This is a particularly interesting walk (or, even better, cycle – however, to bike it, you are supposed to have a permit from the British Waterways Board), as the canal heads up alongside the railway, occasionally being criss-crossed by the Old 'un. A branch loop a few miles on connects with **Edgbaston Reservoir**. A couple of miles farther, after passing the austere and grim Victorian frontage of Winson Green prison, Smethwick's **Galton Valley** is reached. This is an especially deep and noticeably green cutting, crossed by some impressive bridges (including the magnificent **Engine Arm Aqueduct**). The bursts of near-solitude are sporadically shattered by the rusting waterside industry and the adjoining main railway line – although these add to the novelty value of such a find. For details, contact the Galton Valley Centre in Rolfe Street (021-569 3534). The Valley can be directly reached from Smethwick Rolfe Street station or bus 450. Nearby refreshment is provided in the unpretentious M&B pub the **Old Talbot**, opposite Rolfe Street station on Tollhouse Way.

One of the most mind- (and ear-) blowing canal perspectives in Birmingham comes farther down the Birmingham & Fazeley canal, where it meets the Tame Valley and Birmingham & Warwick canals at **Salford Junction** – right under the swirling and overwhelming swoops and spurs of Spaghetti Junction. With the railway whistling past as well, this small, forgotten part of the city really is a microcosm of transport history and achievement. It can be reached via a short walk across Lichfield Road from Aston station, or via buses 65/7, 102/4/5, 114.

In the **Black Country**, canals were as integral to the growth of the area as they were in their easterly neighbour. One of the most fascinating canal trips here is through **Dudley Tunnel**, where the canal cuts under Castle Hill. The tunnel was built without towpaths, wide enough for a single boat. To propel the boat through in pre-motorized days meant two miles of 'legging': lying flat on your back on an outstretched Captain Kidd-style plank and 'walking' sideways along the tunnel walls. Visitors can still have a go. Access is largely through the Black Country Museum (see entry). Other trips are run by the **Dudley Tunnel Trust**. Details on 021-520 5321.

The narrow Dudley Tunnel proved to be too much of a bottleneck in the Black Country canal navigations. To help ease the congestion, the parallel one-and-three-quarter mile **Netherton Tunnel** was built, two boats wide and complete with towpaths. The most interesting part of the tunnel is the southern end, where it emerges into daylight at Windmill End (off St. Peter's Road in Netherton). Here is reclaimed open parkland, dotted with bridges and other remnants from the canal heyday, including **Cobbs Engine House**, an original pumping station built to siphon water out of the mines below. Public-transport access to the park is via buses 276 or 283.

As with nearly all canal-based strolls, one of the best elements is the sheer volume and unique quality of pubs built in close proximity to the waterside. On Windmill End itself is one of 'Mad' O'Rourke's most interesting 'Little pubs' – the **Little Dry Dock**, which serves the usual gargantuan pies and real ales from behind its bar – which is half a narrowboat.

Another notable Black Country canal/pub combination can be found at the **Delph Nine Locks**, rising from Delph Road in Brierley Hill (buses 136/7, 247/8, 292). In fact, there are only eight locks since the canal course was straightened out and strengthened in 1856. Lying snugly under the dominating tower blocks above them, the locks provide an interesting saunter, as well as a good chance to watch sweating boaters struggle up (or down) the hill. At the bottom, Delph Road appears as a surprising Costa del Real Ale, with most local brewers represented in at least one hostelry. Starting by the canal itself, there is the **Tenth Lock** (Banks's – geddit?!), a chintzy emporium that should be avoided at all costs, unless you have a family to seat at one of the canal-side picnic tables. If you're hunting for a pint of Banks's, instead head 50 yards up Delph Roa d to the **Dock and Iron**, a far less pretentious pub. A little farther up still is the **Black Horse** (Courage), and beyond that the **Batham's brewery** and their frontispiece tavern the **Vine** (see also *The Small Breweries* in *MILK AND HONEY*). It is more than worth the five-minute stroll from the canal to reach this pub, a warren of 'back-rooms', snugs, near-perfect ale and excellent food. Entertainment is frequently on in the evenings. The final pub in this long line up Delph Road is the **Ninelocks and Chainmaker** (Davenports). This has been extensively revamped into a steak house family restaurant, with all of the inevitable consequences.

Elsewhere in both Birmingham and the Black Country (and out into the surrounding countryside), walks and boat trips along the confusing pattern of canals offer spectacularly secret places; old wrought iron bridges; dramatic flights of locks and aqueducts. Maps, organized trips and further information are available from the **British Waterways Board** at Auchinleck House, Broad Street, Birmingham B15 1DL (021-633 3666).

See also Birchills Canal Museum in Walsall, in *Museums and Galleries*.

THE 'QUARTERS' OF BIRMINGHAM

Like any fast-growing city, Birmingham's industry evolved into a geographical pattern of different trades. Today, the quarters that these moves produced are frenetically re-inventing themselves and their past as city council and tourism chiefs have cottoned on to the notion of their marketable potential.

One of the most marketable is Birmingham's world-renowned 400-year-old **Jewellery Quarter**, situated around the small streets of Hockley, about half-a-mile north-west of the city centre. So many of the buildings are gleaming with a lick of new paint or pristine brickwork that it is slightly too easy to imagine that you have stepped 'Back In Tyme to Jewellery Industrial Heritage Theme World plc'. But, oh no! The great attraction of the quarter is that it is a vibrant, living industrial and commercial district that, despite extensive sprucing up, still retains a genuine toe-hold in fascinating industrial history, coupled with very many reminders that people are here to Sell, Sell, Sell.

Many of the jewellery firms in the quarter offer tours – it is well worth asking, and trying a couple. Nearly all the shops proclaim that they are the biggest, the best, the oldest or the cheapest. Sometimes, it is true, you can pick up a real bargain. Sometimes, it is equally true, you'd be better off in the Merry Hill Centre.

The heart of the quarter is the clocktower at the crossroads of

Warstone Lane, Frederick and Vyse Streets. Here you'll find the seriously tarted-up **Rose Villa Tavern** (M&B beers), which is as good a place as any to start your exploration. A Jewellery Quarter **Discovery Centre** should be opening near here in 1991, to add to the recent crop of wine bars, bistros and fashion shops. Walking Guides to the district are available in local shops (including *Brumtrail no.6*), or, if you want to get some serious shopping done, consult the *Factory Shop Guide: Western Midlands*, which details some of the best places to pile your pennies into. A taste of the kind of thematic shopping to come is provided by **Spencer's Malls**, between Spencer and Augusta Streets – an upmarket, arty-crafty-jewelly, chic set of shops under one roof. Better bargains are found in the neighbouring streets and alley-ways.

The Jewellery Quarter is the ideal area in which to meander through the streets, window-shop or just soak in the evident history. One way of doing the latter is by taking a tour of the **Assay Office** in Newhall Street (almost opposite the Science Museum). This is the industry's quality control: the hallmarking office. Inside, it's a grand and dignified building that immediately impresses its status and glory on any visitor. Tours are fairly regular. Details on 021-236 6951/2/3.

Inevitably, such a diverse and vibrant neighbourhood attracts a very different workforce as well – especially in the industries of advertising, architecture, finance and the media. This is especially obvious from the glimpses of besuited wunderkinds and flash cars that you get among the flourishing wine bars and trendy eating houses around the old Vittoria Works and the beautifully sedate **St Paul's Square**. Often described in the much over-used – but nonetheless very appropriate - phrase of 'an oasis of peace', Birmingham's only remaining complete Georgian square focuses on the graceful lines of **St Paul's Church**, built as a more modest replica of London's St. Martin-in-the-Fields.

The church is open on Monday, Tuesday, Wednesday and Friday lunchtimes, and is well worth an inspection. Inside, old box pews and magnificent glass provide a superb setting for occasional choral and classical concerts and broadcasts – including many on the restored organ.

Around the square, town houses have effortlessly metamorphosed into bijou watering holes awash with fake Victoriana and plastic potted plants. Every lunchtime and early evening, the sound of braying executives bolstering their expense accounts rents the quiet air of one of the most surprising and interesting districts of the city. Particularly notable examples of the designer bars are **Lloyds off the Square** at 36 Ludgate Hill (which also serves food – but then so does the Wimpy), which is a mock-western, MTV-toting shock to the system; Banks's the **Ropewalk** in the square, proclaiming its kitsch self to be a 'Milestone Tavern', you'll be pleased to hear; the **Square**, which, apparently, is 'Birmingham's most dramatic and sophisticated bar and restaurant' – fancy. Some predominantly foodie places serve excellent meals, as well as buckets of carefully-crafted atmosphere. The **Bucklemaker** at 30, Mary Ann Street is a comparatively simple, sturdy (and pricey) cellar and stripped-floorboard kind of establishment, deservedly reputed for good food and very fine wine. Reserve on 021-200 2515. Other good local foodie joints are the quite pricey **Silverside** 27 Warstone Lane (021-233 3655), the cheaper **Chamberlain's Bistro** in the same street at number 52 (021-236 0400) and **Henry's Cantonese Restaurant** at 27 St Paul's Square (021-200 1136).

The **Chinese Quarter**, around Ladywell Walk and Wrottesley Street at the top of Hurst Street by the Hippodrome, presents a good selection of restaurants, Chinese supermarkets and centres of ancient healing and faith. The city council have designated it a 'Bright Lights' area, which translates into tarting it up and building a couple of pagodas. Details of restaurants in *MILK AND HONEY*.

The city's **Gun Quarter** and **Science Quarter** lie next to each other around Aston University, off the James Watt Queensway. Apart from the **Science Park**, founded in 1982 and now housing over fifty companies, there is a rich mix of the past and the future in the district: the chance to see round some of the ancient gunsmiths, as well as visiting some of the futuristic scientific developments springing up. Most of the remaining gunsmiths are sheltering under St Chad's Queensway around Loveday, Bath and Price Streets. The **Birmingham Gun Barrel Proof House** dates back nearly two centuries and is a fair old stroll away in Banbury Street, near the beautiful old Curzon Street station. The Proof House contains a museum that can be visited by arrangement (021-643 3860).

Just beyond, slightly to the east of the area, lies the biggest piece of urban regeneration in Europe: the 2,300-acre **Heartlands** project. This is based on the suburbs of Vauxhall, Nechells, Bordesley, Duddeston and Saltley, which have suffered many of the most acute problems of Britain's inner-city areas. Eventually, a vast industrial/commercial/residential Nirvana complete with working canal network is envisaged. Heartlands currently resembles (or rather is) one huge building site, and it needs a very vivid imagination (or some illicit substance) to picture what is going to be the great dream-town of the twenty-first century.

Heartlands is an experiment by the UK's first private urban development agency. It is, one could say, a Thatcherite dream – all the more surprising, therefore, that the Labour-controlled Birmingham City Council is such an enthusiastic supporter (and minority shareholder). There are the inevitable controversies surrounding the project, but, hopefully, those involved have learned from the grave mistakes made in similar work in places such as London Docklands. Details of this vast and far-reaching development can be obtained on 021-333 3246.

If urban redevelopment schemes are the bag that you find yourself into (and who doesn't?), the obvious quarter to amble around is that of **Broad Street**, notably the **International Convention Centre**. The area also incorporates Gas Street Basin (see *The Canals*) and the spick new dream-piazza **Centenary Square**, outside the **Repertory Theatre**. Next to the Rep is the impressively dignified white dome of the **Hall of Memory** (key available from neighbouring **Baskerville House**), opposite the shiny new Hyatt Regency Hotel. One of the most interesting areas to discover is around the back of the ICC, backing on to the **National Indoor Sports Arena** and the canals.

The 'Green' West Midlands: Parks and Open Space

More canals than Venice...and more trees than Paris. Oh yes. Birmingham's **Botanical Gardens** on Westbourne Road in Edgbaston (buses 3, 10, 21/2/3/5/9) were established over 150 years ago to provide the more genteel members of Midlands society with a rare tropical area in which to escape and linger. Many of the early gardens and houses remain – among them the Cacti and Succulent House (which sounds like a venue for a *Carry On* film...), a Palm House, Rock Garden, Rhododendron Walk, Aviary and a Garden for the Disabled, comprising many useful and original ideas for people with disabilities. There's also a good tea room. Open every day from 0900 (1000 on Sundays) until dusk or 2000. It costs around £1.50 to get in (with reductions for students and children). As was said in the *Gardeners' Chronicle* of September 1872: 'In the Birmingham Botanic Gardens one feels in the country, far away from the din of commerce, the roar of trade, and the contentions of politics'. Maybe trade isn't roaring quite as ferociously these days, but it's still a tranquil far cry from Five Ways island and the Hagley Road, just hundreds of yards away.

Elsewhere in the second city, there is the truly delightful **Cannon Hill Park** on Edgbaston Road (buses 1, 35, 45/7, 61/2/3, 119, 963), complete with putting, tennis, bowling, boating and children's play areas. It is one of the city's most popular parks, playing host to many festivals and special events throughout the year, including music (jazz especially), play events, an international festival, storytelling, live theatre and a 'Birmingham by the sea' day! The park borders the **river Rea**, which may not be the Thames or the Seine, but which still makes for a pleasant stroll up towards Stirchley. Guided walks and more details of events from the Park Ranger on 021-442 4226.

Part of the attraction of Cannon Hill Park is its proximity to the **Midlands Arts Centre**, the **Edgbaston Cricket Ground** (home of Warwickshire CCC) and the **Birmingham Nature Centre**, on the Pershore Road. Admission to the Nature Centre is free and open from March to November. Inside, kids and older kids will be pleasantly surprised by the wild animals around the site or occasional events such as tortoise MOTs and sheep-shearing. Details on 021-472 7775.

The biggest and greenest city 'lung' in Europe is **Sutton Park**, the 2,500-acre space lying between Sutton Coldfield and Streetly. Public-transport access from Sutton Coldfield railway station, or dozens of buses around the perimeter, serving Sutton, Four Oaks, Kingstanding and Streetly. Whatever your rural desire, you are pretty well guaranteed to be satiated by the choice in Sutton Park. Walks (instructive 'Ranger's Ramble' leaflets available), birdwatching, flowers, fishing, swimming in the open-air lido, wildlife and regular special events throughout all four seasons. The excellent **Visitor Centre** will set you on your way, near the Town Gate in Park Road, Sutton Coldfield. Details of the massive variety of activities on offer on 021-355 6370.

A mile or so to the west of Sutton Park is the surprisingly rural district around **Barr Beacon**, just off the B4151/2 between Walsall and Streetly. The 700-foot-high beacon itself commands spectacular views over the towns and cities of the region and its surrounding countryside. The name has lent itself to the rather anonymous **Beacon Regional Park**, a contrived link-up of patches of greenery snaking through Sandwell and Walsall, right up to Chasewater on the Staffordshire border. Some of the highlights include the **Park Lime Pits**, next to the occasionally sylvan **Rushall Canal**, and the starting point of the regional park, **Sandwell Valley**.

Divided by the roaring M5, the Valley consists of over 2,000 acres of wood, lake and park land, where you can windsurf, golf, canoe, sail or horse-ride, as well as walk, until you drop. The **Sandwell Park Farm**, in the middle of the Valley, is a restored Queen Anne farmhouse (did she ever live in West Brom?), now serving as a livestock and visitor centre. Nearby are the ruins (lately spruced up and with a few ghostly waxwork monks lurking in the shadows) of **Sandwell Priory**. The Valley hosts a **Sports Festival** in June and July, as well as the annual August Bank Holiday **Sandwell Show**, a rare riot of fun, live music, a fair, horsey events, twinky arty-crafty goods and loads of screaming children. Public transport: Hamstead railway station on the Walsall line and then a mile walk, or buses 16, 17, 406, 451, 632, 651. More details from the Visitor Centre on 021-553 0220/2147 or the R.S.P.B. reserve and Nature Centre (Tanhouse Avenue off B4167 Hamstead Road) on 021-358 3013.

For something a little more formal, a historic seventeenth- and eighteenth-century walled garden can be seen at the **Castle Bromwich Hall Gardens**, off Chester Road (021-749 4100). Try and close your ears to the historical sound of junction five of the M6 but a couple of hundred yards away.

For those of an aquatic bent, **Edgbaston Reservoir** is the nearest we can offer to Lake Garda or the Caspian Sea. It's a popular little haunt with all kinds of folk – from panting joggers to the weekend fishing brigade. Access is via Reservoir Road, Edgbaston (no surprise there) - near bus routes 8 and 43. Just up the road lies one of the earliest municipal open spaces, **Summerfield Park**, dating from 1876.

Very near Yardley Wood station (and bus routes 12, 13, 69) lies **Trittiford Mill Park**, straddling the (fairly) verdant banks of the River Cole. The park is dominated by the Mill Pool, which attracts interesting wildlife (including bats), as well as some strapping canoeists. There's also an interesting walk up the Cole through the attractively-named **Dingles Recreation Ground**. Mind you don't step in too many Dingles...

The deserved pride of **Walsall** is its **Arboretum** (a short walk from Walsall station or any bus serving the town centre). Here you can wander free as a birdie in beautifully laid-out grounds containing the most spectacular selection of trees and lakes. The explosion of colour in autumn can lead you to believe that someone has spiked your drink with something illegal. And, if that's not enough, Walsall council lay on extensive autumn evening illuminations: over 60,000 light bulbs, lasers, a fairground and music every night from the end of August through to mid-October. Details on 0922-21205.

Other city parks worth a meander through include **Handsworth Park** on Grove Lane in Handsworth (buses 16, 16A, 76), which stages the brilliant annual carnival; **Calthorpe Park**, just off the Pershore Road and Edward Road between Edgbaston and Balsall Heath, a fine example of Victorian industrial philanthropy in the Cadbury vein (buses X6, 45/7); the ornate **Aston Park**, encircling and complementing Aston Hall (see page 60); **Wren's Nest Nature Reserve** (buses 126, 581) on Wren's Hill

Road in Dudley is a geologist's dream, as well as offering extensive views over the Black Country.

Lying on the fringes of the big smoke are a number of semi-rural areas popular with stampeding hordes of weekend Brummies. The **Lickey Hills**, on the edge of Rubery in south-west Birmingham rise to over 800 feet, giving a toytown panorama of the city (best from Beacon Hill), as well as loads of rivers, streams and walks. Access is from the B4096 (Rose Hill) and B4120 (Lickey Road) or bus 62, 145, 202/3/4. Barnt Green station lies at the southern end of the hills, about two miles away. Just the other side of the A38 lies the **Waseley Hills Country Park** (buses 49, 61, 202/3/4, 963), bursting with marshes, views, birds, rabbits, bluebells, ponds and the odd Diet Tango can.

Woodgate Valley, a thin finger of rural calm between the sprawling post war developments of California and Ridgacre in west Birmingham, offers many a rustic pastime for tree-starved townies. The Visitor Centre and refreshment rooms are on Clapgate Lane, near Lapal (buses 23, 86). Facilities for people with disabilities are good, including cassette guides for the visually impaired, and donkey-drawn rides for those with walking problems. Pony trekking is also available. Details of the Visitor Centre on 021-422 2400 or 021-421 7575.

The **Clent Hills** are slightly farther out (just south of Halesowen), although well worth the trip (a brisk hike from the bus stop on the A456, where Midland Red Birmingham -- Kidderminster buses stop, or buses 318/9, 320 to Clent Holy Cross from Stourbridge). The views over the Worcestershire countryside, Birmingham and neighbouring Hagley Hall are just reward for the fairly hefty climb. **Clent** village nestles among the hills, and is a thoroughly satisfying foil to the excesses of exercise, especially if you spend your hours in the snug of the excellent **Vine** pub.

Other Ideas to get you out

The **Birmingham City Sightseeing Tour** is a great way to find out things about the city from a purpose-designed bus tour. Two different ones are offered: a two-hour tour of the city centre, the canals and the jewellery quarter or an all-day tour of Manors, Mills and Mansions. They leave from the WMT Travel Shop in Colmore Row (021-200 3334), and are bookable there or at the Ticket Shop, City Arcade (021-643 2514). Alternatively, you could construct your own tour with a day bus pass – or spend an hour or two on the infamous No.11 bus **Outer Circle** route, which passes through all of the most interesting parts of the city on the outskirts of the city centre.

Being a **TV** or **radio audience** for one of the multitude of shows that are produced in Birmingham is fun, free and gives you a chance to see what a stage-managed procedure spontaneity really is. Contact **BBC Pebble Mill** on 021-414 8888 or **Central Independent Television** on 021-643 9898.

A rather expensive treat would be to hire your own **hot air balloon** for a casual glide over the region. The major company that offers this is Champagne Flights International at Roman House, Newport Road, Albrighton, near Wolverhampton. Ring them on 0902-373293 for more details on how to become airborne.

Just outside Stourbridge is the village of **Hagley**, complete with its superb Palladian **Hall**. To try and keep aristocratic body and soul together, the Cobhams, owners of the place, have turned it into an upmarket conference centre and amusement park. One regular event that may amuse, all the same, is their **murder evening**, where you have to try and fathom out why these poor frustrated actors keep dropping head first into the vichyssoise. Again, very expensive, but worth it for a special occasion. Details on 0562-882408.

Festivals and Special Events

THE FESTIVALS

There has been a great national tendency in recent years to bung a few cryptically connected events together in one month and brashly declare it to be a festival. Birmingham especially has ploughed much of its artistic reputation into such events, although many of these have developed from small beginnings and become national leaders in their field. They have largely grown out of existing activity in the city, which the council have recognized and co-ordinated, as part of their heartfelt belief in the power of the arts to bring cultural development.

The award-winning **International Film & TV Festival** (September/ October) contains a couple of weeks of screenings, debates and premières that draws many of the biggest names in the 'meeja' world to the city. The festival is characterized by some imaginative programming. Another festival that has become nationally famous is the **Jazz Festival** (July), whose size and popularity has soared in the years since its low-key inception as a one-day jamming session in Cannon Hill Park in 1984.

The Birmingham **Readers and Writers** Festival (March) is the only urban-based literature festival in the UK. Most such events take place in the sylvan surroundings of Welsh hills or southern coastal plains, and Birmingham's entry into the fray brought only characteristic sneering from the literary establishment. This has now evaporated into muted universal praise for an unpretentious festival, which draws in the glittering literati as well as the ordinary readers.

A new Birmingham festival is the three-day **Storytelling** event in late July throughout MAC and Cannon Hill Park. The first one, in 1990, was a great success, managing to stick to its exciting aims of rejuvenating the dying culture of verbal storytelling. This is achieved through theatre, art, workshops and readings covering the vast international sphere from Celtic legends to Caribbean Ananse and Trickster tales. Events in the park are free, although you have to pay for those in MAC.

As if all this wasn't enough, the well-established **International Women's Festival** in March now takes over huge swathes of the city during its short annual life. Theatre, dance, comedy, art, workshops, health and conferences combine to bring a rare cosmopolitan feel to many of the city's venues.

Wolverhampton saw its first ever festival in October 1990, something that will no doubt become a regular annual feature. As the Chair of the Council's Leisure Services Committee admits in the introduction to the Festival brochure: 'The origin of the Festival is quite unconventional, for it came about as the result of a search by Harp Premier Export Lager to find a town, willing and able to host a wide range of events which they would part sponsor'. Despite its decided lack of community roots, the Festival encompasses a wide range of events throughout the town, and, as a first attempt, it is quite impressive.

Other recent first attempts that will no doubt become bigger and bigger as the years drag by are the **Sandwell Arts Festival**, the first of which was held in October 1990, **Walsall Leather Festival**, which may sound like every kink's dream bank holiday, but which is in fact, a series of events loosely connected by the town's staple industry.

SUPER PRIX

Birmingham City Council's desperation to catapult itself on to the international stage with 'prestige' events has been exemplified in the annual August Bank Holdiay road race. This is a bold – but surely ultimately frivolous – attempt to link Brum with cities such as Monte Carlo in the world's mind. Considering the cost, and the fact that unlike the festivals the benefits for the good folk of the city are a little harder to see, the Super prix arouses very mixed emotions – especially for those who live within ear-splitting distance of the track.

The Super prix has had an ignominious history: washed out by a hurricane in its first year, the city council claim that it has gone from strength to strength, despite tumbling attendances in recent years. The deal with the Formula 3000 racers came to an end in 1990, but the council are single-mindedly pursuing alternatives for coming years. Details on the Motor Race Unit at the Council House on 021-235 2026.

THE NATIONAL EXHIBITION CENTRE (NEC)

The NEC was established in south-east Birmingham in 1976 as Britain's largest exhibition complex. Since then, it has undergone massive expansion, aiming ultimately to double in size by the year 2004. Currently it consists of eight main halls: the Arena (chiefly used for concerts), the Gallery, Atrium and Forum adding up to 100,000 square metres of space. No doubt building will be forced to cease when the few remaining euphemisms for hall have been exhausted.

Despite this huge expanse (and indeed expense – the £50-million loan is backed by Birmingham City Council), the NEC has rather less than one might expect to offer the general public. The majority of staged events are trade-only fairs or company seminars and AGMs. Such public events as there are can be subdivided into three areas.

- ***Exhibitions*** ranging from Racing Pigeons to Holiday & Travel, from Careers to Retirement. To further boost its leading status, the NEC now hosts the biennial Motor Show (next in 1992), Crufts Dog Show and the BBC Clothes Show exhibition. All these were previously held in London.
- ***Sporting events*** including basketball, gymnastics, motorcross, the Royal International Horse Show and skating (ranging from Walt Disney on Ice to the 1989 European Figure Skating Championships). All in the Arena. Box office and more information on 021-780 4133.
- ***Concerts*** are also held in the cavernous Arena, which seats about 12,000. Ticket prices range from £8 upwards depending on the mega status of the megastar concerned. It's a popular venue with Big Names who deign to give the whole of Eng-Land just one night of their precious time, due to its central location. Sitting at the back or sides can generate as much atmosphere as you'd find in the average train spotters' convention, so it's worth getting a standing ticket to be at the front.

Transport to the NEC complex is uncommonly simple. Most direct is the train (Inter-City or local from New Street, Sandwell & Dudley, Wolverhampton) to Birmingham International station, slap next to the halls of the Exhibition Centre. Numerous buses and coaches also serve it.

For Kids

PLACES TO GO

History and Horticulture

One of the classic days out that has entertained kids for a couple of generations is **Dudley Castle and Zoo** (0384-252401). £3.00 for adults, £1.50 for kids or family ticket £8.50. The zoo certainly looks tattier than you may remember from childhood, although there's still plenty to learn, especially with Dudley's new-found status as the self-styled Disneyworld of the West Midlands, complete with the neighbouring **Geochrom** (the 'zoo of the future' in a vast glass dome) and Black Country Museum (021-557 9643).

Sandwell Park Farm is a working Victorian farm and museum that gives those poor city slickin' kids a chance to watch a few animals copulate in that thar natural way. See *The 'Green' West Midlands*. One of the best free days out is in Sedgley, three miles north-west of Dudley, where you'll find the **Cotwall End Nature Reserve** on Catholic Lane (near the routes of buses 558 and 566). Here you'll see rare breeds of wildfowl, wild beasts and farm animals as well as very common breeds of ice cream and picnic areas. There are pools, walks, forest land, a craft centre and a children's play area for streetwise kids who hate old Mother Nature. Annually on the first Sunday in September, the reserve hosts the blandly titled **Country Day**, with lots of games, music, crafts and dancing with an olde-time yokel feel.

In Hockley's All Saints Street, the **Port '86** park (021-551 4837) boasts an adventure playground, a farm and a mural that children can practise their early graffiti tendencies on. Short trips on the canal are also available, as are horse- and pony-riding for children with disabilties. Part of a Community Education Programme, Port 86 also has a latchkey scheme. Bus 96. Other city places where the children can get a bit mucky and learn a little greenness in the process are the **South Aston Community Park** in Upper Sutton Street, Aston, 021-359 4133, (bus 8 or any bus up the Lichfield Road and Walsall Road), the **British Trust for**

Conservation Volunteers at the Conservation Centre, 52 Firsby Road in Quinton, 021-426 5588, (bus 10), the **Lifford Water Triangle** on the Reservoir, Tunnel Lane, off Lifford Lane (buses 11, 45, 47, 35), a water world where the canal, the river Rea and the reservoir meet, offering many projects on the banks.

St Paul's Venture includes a City Farm with some goats, gerbils, sheep, ducks and donkey rides in the heart of Balsall Heath, in Malvern Street, off Clifton Road, 021-440 4232 (bus 50). There's also a City Farm at **Holy Trinity**, Cooksey Road, Small Heath (021-772 0184). Similarly rural, even if it is in the slipstream of Birmingham Airport, is the **Sheldon Country Park** (021-742 0226), based at the Old Rectory Farm, Ragley Drive, off Church Road in Sheldon (bus 60). In the same muddy vein, take the bus 129 or the No.11 bus circular to the Urban Wildlife Trust's **Deersleap Wood** in Portland Road, Bearwood.

Parks and **open spaces** are more comprehensively covered in '*JOY RIDES*', although it is impossible to go into detail about the 200 plus parks in the region. Dozens of them have play huts or areas within them – most notably the brand-new adventure playground in **Cannon Hill Park**, complete with ace adventure rides and climbs in a setting that suits people of all ages. **Kings Heath Park**, Vicarage Road, has an animal enclosure, **Senneleys Park**, Senneleys Park Road, Bartley Green, a BMX track (which also stages occasional big events), **Swanshurst Park**, Swanshurst Lane, Kings Heath, a boating pool and **Valley Parkway**, Bournville Lane, a yachting pool for miniature boats.

On the edge of Cannon Hill Park is the noted **MAC**, which contains all kinds of arty treats for little Jasmin and Jeremy, as well as the internationally famous **Cannon Hill Puppet Theatre**, offering sophisticated puppet entertainment targeted at a range of ages. It is not being immodest in advertising itself as the Midlands' premier venue – go seek. Details on 021-440 3838.

Birmingham's central **Museum and Art Gallery** lay on some excellent entertainments for children, as well as having a shop stocking a host of ideas for days out and activities for the easily bored smaller members of the household.

An excellent (and free) museum for all sizes and shapes of people is the Birmingham **Museum of Science and Industry** in Newhall Street (021-236 1022) – see *Museums and Galleries*.

Sport

Most of the things that can keep the whole family happy are covered in the separate section on sport throughout the region. The **Ackers Trust** in Golden Hillock Road, Small Heath (021-771 4448), is a particularly exciting multi-adventure park for all ages. The **Birmingham Wheels Park** in Adderley Road South, Saltley, offers bikes, BMX, road cycle circuits and other wheelie-based ventures for kids aged eleven and upwards. Details on 021-771 0725.

Swimming is an excellent, fairly cheap sport that should be fun for all. Your nearest pool can be found under your borough council entry in the telephone directory. Courses for the under fives are held at the **Charles Gillet Centre** at Selly Oak College, 998 Bristol Road (021-472 4231) – but the waiting list is always huge.

If you're reaching screaming point, it is worth getting in touch with your **local council**. All in the region offer a plethora of holiday-time activities that are guaranteed to keep the little loves amused. One of the most imaginative is the summertime **Birmingham Adventure Game**. Here the children shell out a couple of quid to get a 'passport', which enables them to free bus travel and free entry to dozens of places throughout the city. At each one they perform a challenge, which could win them a prize. Participants include many local sports centres, TV and radio stations, environmental groups and museums. It's an excellent and thoroughly entertaining way to learn about the hidden corners of your own city. Details on 021-235 3943 or from the City Council Recreation & Community Services Department. Details of this and all local council initiatives from your local library.

Also available from your library is an excellent book, *Birmingham for the Under-fives*, produced in 1985 and hence often out of date. Nonetheless, it's full of good ideas though it covers only the area of Birmingham City Council.

SHOPPING AND TOWN CENTRES

In the major shopping areas, places to keep the children amused include the horrendously titled **Kiddies Korner** in the Central Court of the **Bull Ring** Shopping Centre, which charges a small fee for the childcare provision offered (details on 021-643 8880) and a children's play area and supervised crèche in the **Merry Hill** centre.

Birmingham city centre is now offering some innovative **Father and Baby rooms** dotted at strategic points, at long last recognizing that it's not only mothers that have to drag the kids round the sales.

Birmingham city centre's many markets are good for children's clothes and toys, as well as grabbing a cheap snack. Details of these and many of the other shopping centres throughout the region are in *Shopping* in *LEISURE TIME*. Birmingham and Wolverhampton centres, and the Merry Hill Centre in Brierley Hill have the most comprehensive range of shops to suit.

ORGANIZATIONS

Gingerbread (national organization for one-parent families) Church Centre, Carrs Lane, Birmingham B4 7SX (021-631 2103).

5. THE TWILIGHT ZONE

A Voyage Round My Handbag: Clubs and Music Venues

NIGHTCLUBS

The standard of most of the West Midlands' nightclubs is more or less that of a swamp. Most have particular dress codes (no jeans, no trainers, gents with a tie, ladies' white stilettos and Elastoplast on the heel guarantees a free glass of Babycham etc.) and play a thumpy selection of chart-based dross.

Rising above the quagmire is the new **Institute**, in the old Digbeth Civic Hall (opposite the coach station). Decorated in a surprisingly tasteful combination of orange, purple and green, it contains a wide variety of different floors and corners. It is also the only club in town which you can enter wearing a pair of jeans. Inside there is The Dance Factory, a bare street playing vicious music; the main Forum, which is the converted main arena of the Civic Hall (the municipal organ is still in place); a refreshing no-smoking New Orleans-style jazz club; and a regular comedy club with some of the biggest names from the London circuit.

The Institute offers regular live bands and 'themed' music nights (e.g. Latin, World, Soul) as well as vegetarian, Russian and French restaurants. There is a minimum entrance fee of £4 at the weekend. Details on 021-643 7788.

Le Click Club at **Burberries** (220 Broad Street, 021-643 1500) on a Tuesday night is Brum's major indie venue, having spawned some of the region's most notable bands of recent years. The rest of the week at Burberries is eminently missable.

Other city centre major clubs are of a rather samey ilk: the revolting **Pagoda Park** in Smallbrook Queensway (021-643 6696), **Liberty's** at 184 Hagley Road (021-454 4444), **XLs** in Auchinleck Square, Five Ways (021-643 9433) and **The Dome** in the Horsefair (021-622 2233). During the week these are generally full of drunk businessmen searching for a quick leg-over, and, at weekends, their younger Brummie counterparts. **Ritzy's**, in Hurst Street (021-643 4715), rose in its kitsch way from the ashes of the troubled, but usually worthwhile, Powerhouse. A great shame.

The slightly less cringeworthy converted canal-side warehouse **Bobby Brown's The Club** in Gas Street (021-643 2573) is worth a closer look, as is the essentially scruffy, but quite enjoyable, **Goldwyns** in Suffolk Place (021-643 6843). Many of the above offer weekday student nights, where the dress code is relaxed a bit, the music is generally more thought- (and dance-) provoking than the Friday night endless chart pap, and the drinks are a little less expensive. However, for those working, boogieing your socks off until the early hours on a Tuesday has its drawbacks....

For those seeking a harmonious evening of pure metal from bands with names like Angst Thrash or Death By Vomit, **Edwards No. 8** in Lower Severn Street, off John Bright Street (021-643 5835), is the place to rupture your eardrums in. They also host some good dance nights. In Regents Park Road, Small Heath, the **Porsche** club (021-773 5958) puts on some excellent club nights.

The **Moseley Dance Centre** has been at the forefront of new music in the region: it plays regular host to Latin, soul, bongo-go and house bands and nights, including popular **raves** on Saturday nights; 572 Moseley Road, Balsall Heath/Moseley (021-449 0779). **Acafess** at 198 Moseley Road, Highgate (021-440 5288) puts on some fine events to get your feet a-tapping, and raves are held at the **Winson Green Community Centre** in Winson Green Road. In the heart of the Jewellery Quarter, **Branstons**, in Branston Street (021-236 6362), offers stirring soul, funk and jazz nights. World music also features highly in the sweaty **Piccadilly** and **West End Bar** at the end of Colmore Row on St. Chad's Queensway (021-236 2435).

Other towns in the region suffer from an acute lack of decent clubs beyond pubs with discos or live music. **Walsall** and **Dudley** both have a **JBs** (see below); Dudley also has **Cromwells** on Castle Hill (0384-455806). For a town so large, **Wolverhampton** fares little better, with **Ritzy's** in Showell Road, Bushbury (0902-773669) and **Scruples** on the Birmingham Road (0902-53754). The names alone should whisper a warning to more sensitive spirits although Ritzy's has the almost institutionalized Tuesday night for the relatively indie music and cheaper entry for students, and – shock horror! – for just this one night a week 'stylish denims will be OK'. Hold back if you can. **Monaco** at 50 Worcester Street, Wolverhampton (0902-26690), is a little more varied in its selection, hosting nights of indie music, soul, hip-hop, reggae, r'n'b, jazz and sokka among others.

LIVE MUSIC: ROCK AND POP

The West Midlands was briefly the focal point of British music during the ska and two-tone surge in 1980. Briefly is most certainly the operative word here – although there has always been a steady stream of good home-grown music that has spawned talents as diverse as Roy Wood and Wizzard, Slade, Duran Duran, UB40, the Electric Light Orchestra, Led Zeppelin, Joan Armatrading, Fuzzbox and The Wonder Stuff.

For all flavours of live music, many of the pubs in the area have occasional or regular bands of varying degrees of quality – some of the major ones are included here, many of the others are covered in the section on pubs.

Mega gigs are held at the **National Exhibition Centre** (see *Festivals and Special Events*), where most seats seem to have been bought by corporate hospitality groups wooing bemused Japanese businessmen. General enquiries on 021-780 4141, box office 021-780 4133.

Until 1987, the **Birmingham Odeon** played host to most of the big bands visiting the region. Then, it suddenly decided to go back to being just a cinema, leaving quite a void to fill for a good, general large venue that wasn't as cavernous and devoid of atmosphere as the NEC. The nearest to filling this void have been venues like the **Hummingbird** in Dale End, at the top of the High Street, a (supposedly) 2,000-capacity venue that has a packed menu of reggae and indie bands on regularly. Details on 021-236 4236.

The **Irish Centre** and its **Downliners** R'n'B club in Digbeth belies its appearance of a church hall, putting on regular gigs of great sweaty popularity. One of the city's most underrated venues (021-622 2314/2332), which is currently being renovated.

Many multi-use venues host regular rock concerts, including Birmingham **Town Hall, MAC** (formerly the Midlands Arts Centre) and Wolverhampton's **Civic Hall**.

Well out of the way at 1652 Pershore Road in Cotteridge is the brilliant **Breedon Bar** (021-4590 6573), which puts on a staggering array of inspired live music. It's also a very pleasant place to have a relaxed bevvy. Another regular and occasionally superb venue is the **Barrel Organ** in Digbeth (021-622 1353).

In Dudley, **JBs** club in King Street (0384-253597) hosts regular live bands, interspersed with some pretty dodgy clubbing. Their counterpart, **JBs at Junction 10** at 10 Bentley Road South on the outskirts of Walsall (0922-648100), has a similar menu.

News of much of the region's vibrant rock scene is contained within the excellent free monthly *Brum Beat* ('The Music Mag of the Midlands'), which can be picked up at record shops, tourist offices and arts venues throughout the region.

LIVE MUSIC: JAZZ AND FOLK

As well as the big venues such as MAC, the Adrian Boult Hall and the Wolverhampton Civic Hall, there are a good few jazz and folk pubs and clubs throughout the region. Just off the Hagley Road, in Waterworks Road, Ladywood, is the **Waterworks Club**, with excellent live jazz and bar extension on Monday nights. Details on 021-454 0212. The **Cannonball** on the corner of Adderley Street and Liverpool Street (021-772 1403) in Bordesley ends up most nights with some excellent and very informal jam sessions in a sea of jazz memorabllia. **Acafess**, (see *MILK AND HONEY*) in Highgate, have regular jazz nights in among the myriad of other musical events.

The **Bear Tavern** (021-429 1184) in Bearwood Road, Bearwood, is an excellent and lively pub that frequently has good jazz on in the evening. They are also the Wednesday night hosts of the XXXX Cabaret. Details on 021-429 1184. The **Porsche** club in Regents Park Road, Small Heath (021-772 6024) hosts regular weekend jazz and reggae gigs.
In Bilston, near Wolverhampton, the aptly named **Trumpet** puts on nightly jazz to combine with some excellent Holden's beer. Music on Sunday lunchtimes too (0902-493723). A slightly larger regular Sunday lunchtime venue is the **Strathallan Hotel** at 225 Hagley Road, Edgbaston (021-455 9777). The **Hen and Chickens** in Wolverhampton Road, Oldbury (021-552 1058), puts on occasional jazz extravaganzas, as well as some other regular musical thrills. Walsall's **Crest Hotel** in Birmingham Road (0922-33555) has jazz evenings every Tuesday and Thursday.

The **Birmingham International Jazz Festival** has grown cataclysmically from a one-day jam session in Cannon Hill Park in 1984 into a packed, ten-day event attracting people from all over the world. Taking place in early July, pubs, parks, shopping centres, even car showrooms throughout the region burst into life with literally hundreds of events to suit all tastes and pockets. Even Digbeth coach station is used! The live jazz bus also tours around the city, bringing its organized chaos to many local districts. The Festival Office is at PO Box 944, Edgbaston, Birmingham B16 8UT. Hotline on 021-454 7020.

In Walsall, the best and most regular jazz venue is the Wharf Bar of the **Crest Hotel** on the A34 Birmingham Road (0922-33555). Sunday lunchtime entertainment is on at the **Walsall Arms** in Bank Street (0922-

26660). In Brierley Hill, the excellent Batham's flagship pub the **Vine** (or **Bull & Bladder**) in Delph Road puts on regular folk and jazz nights in the near-perfect setting.

Jazz Information on 021-559 6205 (daytime) and 0902-764332 (evening). There is also the free quarterly newspaper *Jazz in the Midlands*, which probably explains what it's for. You can pick it up at most venues and shops.

For a good selection of Arran jumpers, the **Woodman Folk Club** at the Woodman Inn, Mount Pleasant, Kingswinford, near Stourbridge happens every Friday night (0384-273868). Birmingham's **Bell and Pump** club is the city's major folk venue at 20 Waterworks Road, Edgbaston (021-454 0212).

LIVE MUSIC: CLASSICAL

OK, OK, so there's the **City of Birmingham Symphony Orchestra**, led by the unbelievably popular and awesomely talented Simon Rattle. The city are so keen to keep Rattle within their clutches that they have built him a multi-million pound, acoustically perfect **Symphony Hall**, within the new International Convention Centre complex. The CBSO will be playing both here and at the magnificent **Birmingham Town Hall**, with one of the biggest organs you'll ever see, missus. Occasional joint concerts with the **City of Birmingham Choir**, including the notable carol concert. Box office at the Town Hall: 021-236 2392/3889, Symphony Hall 'Hotline': 021-782 8282 and the CBSO registered office for general enquiries: 021-236 1555.

The **Birmingham Conservatoire**, a varied collection of chamber and orchestra musicians, are the CBSO's neighbours in the Adrian Boult Hall, Paradise Place, where they perform most of their work. Many of their performances are at lunchtime, and are free. Tickets from the Town Hall Box Office (see above) or information on 021-331 5908/9. They are also occasional performers at the **Birmingham and Midland Institute** (BMI), a genteel enclave of sophistication in the heart of the city in Margaret Street (021-236 3591). Much of the music laid on is at lunchtimes to attract workers and shoppers – there is a restaurant in the basement open to all concert-goers.

As so few people live in Birmingham city centre, it is hardly surprising that much of the best music is laid on at lunchtimes. The elegant settings of **Birmingham Cathedral** (021-236 6323) and the **Town Hall** (021-236 2392) are used for such concerts regularly, as is the graceful **St Paul's Church** (021-236 7858) on the edge of the Jewellery Quarter.

Refreshments on sale – a pleasant and very cultured alternative to a quick Whopper.

Information on most concerts and theatre from the **Ticket Shop** line on 021-643 2514. Students get substantial discounts on most performances.

A more eclectic brand of classical music can be found at the old Stourbridge Canal Company building, the **Bonded Warehouse** in Canal Street, Stourbridge (0384-395216). Here you could spend an evening tapping your toe to an Elizabethan madrigal, a hurdy-gurdy recital or a recorder workshop. Forsooth.

Classical concerts are also put on with support from local councils, often in town halls (Walsall, Stourbridge, Wolverhampton and Dudley are particularly regular). Ring the local Tourist Information Centre or council office for details.

The Arts and Entertainments

Beyond the pubs, clubs and music venues there is plenty a-happening on the streets of the mean Midlands.

THEATRE

Birmingham boldly proclaims that it has the `greatest concentration of live theatre outside the West End'. This ranks alongside other claims such as that the Dome is `the most impressive nightclub in the world' and that the Pavilions was European Shopping Centre of the year. However, there are a quite a few pearls to snuffle around for.

Birmingham City Centre

The Big Three are the Rep, the Alex and the Hippo. The **Birmingham Repertory Theatre** has undergone a significant recent renaissance to match its newly glamorous neighbours, the International Convention Centre and the landscaped Centenary Square on Broad Street. Productions are held in the huge main theatre and the more experimental studio. The resident company are frequently joined by top touring companies. If all else fails, there's always the excellent Rep Café Bar, with frequent live music and every kind of trendy, tasteless El Salvadorean lager in town. To complete the picture, Sunday nights often see comedy, cabaret or jazz. Plans are afoot to put a canopy over part of the Square to extend the café into the realms of the continental. Good access for people with disabilties, infra-red hearing loops and signed performances for deaf people for each new production at reduced prices. 24-hour information and booking service on 021-236 4455.

The **Alexandra Theatre** in Suffolk Street (021-633 3325) makes repeated efforts to update and face-lift itself, with stunning lack of results. They are the base for the **D'Oyly Carte Opera Company** and endless rounds of solid trad. Gilbert & Sullivan. Most of the rest of the stuff is very commercial musicals and Radio 2 concerts, with the odd flash of good visiting theatre companies.

The 2,000-seat **Birmingham Hippodrome** recently pulled off the very well-publicized coup of bringing the former Sadler's Wells Royal Ballet up the M1 to be based here. They are now renamed the **Birmingham Royal Ballet**. For the rest of the time (and that's 47 weeks of the year) the Hippo puts on the huge shows, pantos and comedies. It is also the English base for the **Welsh National Opera**. In Hurst Street, 021-622 7486.

Above the Hippodrome is the renowned **Dance Centre**, which caters for all kinds of hoofers, looking to improve their steps (and, quite often, their figure). Details on 021-622 3253.

The **Crescent Theatre** in Cumberland Street (off Broad Street) puts on far less grandiose and commercially obvious productions than its near-neighbours. Despite being largely amateur, the standard of performances is high. Details on 021-643 5858.

The **Old Rep** theatre, set among the sleazy cinemas in Station Street, alongside New Street station, is owned and run by the Birmingham & District Theatre Guild. Its diet is a varied one. Details on 021-235 4682.

The **Josiah Mason** Theatre, next to the Central Library in Chamberlain Square, puts on occasional ethnic and fringe events. Details on 021-235 3586.

The Birmingham Convention and Visitor Bureau operate a central **ticket shop** for access to most of the city's big attractions. Available at the Tourist Information Centres in the City Arcade or at the NEC (021-643 2514). They also operate an **information line** for details of hotels, events, places and a bit of culture thrown in. The line in itself is entertainment enough, as you are instructed by Jasper Carrott in a quickfire way to respond to a succession of questions and bleeps in order to establish the information that you are seeking. Try it on 0839-333999.

Outer Birmingham and Sutton Coldfield

The multi-use **MAC** in Edgbaston's Cannon Hill Park presents a wide range of touring theatre companies that should succeed in pleasing an awful lot of people at least some of the time. Theatre, dance-drama, cabaret, music, workshops, international and many events from the various city festivals (readers & writers, jazz, storytelling, classical, women's, film & TV) as well as an excellent programme of classes and teaching – especially in dance. Some of the events spill out into the lovely surroundings of Cannon Hill Park.

MAC is also the base for the deservedly renowned **Cannon Hill Puppet Theatre**, which puts on a huge number of shows targeted at specific age groups, usually up to eleven (although most adults find it intriguing too!). The **Dance Depot**, also part of MAC, runs a vast range of classes covering dance from ballet to flamenco, for people from pregnant women to kids. Since recent revamping, MAC really is the premier Midlands arts venue. Details on 021-440 4221.

The Cave at 516 Moseley Road, between Balsall Heath and Moseley, succeeds in putting on a great variety of shows, many of which examine aspects of Black theatre. Details on 021-440 3742.

The **Highbury Little Theatre** in Sheffield Road, Sutton Coldfield (021-373 2761) is mainly amateur, with occasional visits from professional groups. They operate a very participative policy, running a youth theatre and encouraging people to design, act, direct, light, market or whatever dramaturgical bag you happen to be into. Near Chester Road station.

The **Hall Green Little Theatre** has a similar policy to its sibling in posher Sutton. It's in Pemberley Road, Acock's Green (near Spring Road station). Details on 021-706 1541.

Other theatres with local and amateur productions of varying glitter and a ready cast of frustrated accountants include the **New King's Theatre** in Hampstead Road, Great Barr (021-358 0333) and the **Sutton Arts Theatre** in Sutton Coldfield's South Parade (021-355 5355).

Deep in the heart of the truest, bluest Solihull is the **Library Theatre** in Homer Road (021-704 6962), hosting some major companies such as the Royal National Theatre, as well as a plethora of minor stars.

Wolverhampton and the Black Country

The **Grand Theatre** in Lichfield Street, Wolverhampton town centre, is one of the region's major theatres, well on the up-and-up after near-closure. The mixture of events that they host can really only be described as eclectic: naff pantos with minor soap stars or Cannon and Ball lying cheek by jowl with the Royal Shakespeare Company, some terribly serious Lorca play or a morsel of highbrow ballet. Box office and information on 0902-29212.

Wolves Polytechnic's **Arena Theatre** in Wulfruna Street is used more as a fringe space, with some excellent home-grown and touring productions (box office: 0902-313001, extension 2380). Some performances by travelling companies are held in the **Wulfrun Hall**, Mitre Fold and **Civic Hall**, North Street, bang in Wolverhampton town centre (0902-312030). These are particularly notable for music (from the Pogues to the Philharmonic) and dance.

Occasional theatrical productions (of the rather obvious, but nevertheless enjoyable, variety) take place alfresco in the dramatic setting of **Dudley Castle**. More information on 0384- 250333.

Other local centres of amateur thespian excellence are the **Oldbury Repertory Theatre** in Spring Walk, Langley (021-552 2761), the **Dudley Little Theatre** at the **Netherton Arts Centre**, next to the library on Northfield Road in central Netherton (0384- 254355 for more information) and some performances at **Dudley Town Hall** in St James's Road (0384-456000).

CABARET AND COMEDY

The clubs of the Midlands are just beginning to establish themselves on the cabaret circuit, which has hitherto stuck to being 49 weeks a year in London and three in Edinburgh. The only real home-made comedy that can be seen are the various themes on a **Black Country Night Out**. Even these have been slightly bastardized into neatly packaged lumps of Heritage, especially at **Grorty's Variety Theatre**, 4 Yarley Street, Stambermill, Stourbridge (0384-893441). Here you'll find a permanent nostalgia trip for the days of the Black Country of yore, complete with faggots un' paeze, spotted dick, Aynuk & Ayli entertainment and local comedians. They also run beer tours (returning to the theatre for food and cabaret). The other permanent home of the Night Out is the **Citizens' Theatre** at the Robin Hood, Merry Hill (0384-77756), which is more like a working men's club and far more genuine as a result. Many venues in the region (pubs, town and civic halls and the Black Country Museum among others) host regular Black Country specials – read *What's On* or the *Express and Star* for details. The **Comedy Club** at Mount Pleasant in Bilston (0902-354885) has a varied menu of Black

Country humour, national and international comedians with a sprinkling of cabaret music and meals in baskets.

There are not too many regular comedy venues for cabaret artists playing the Midlands. Large multi-purpose centres that do put on cabaret are those such as **MAC** in Cannon Hill Park (021-440 4221), the **Birmingham Repertory Theatre** in Broad Street (021-236 4455), the **Institute**, Digbeth (021-643 7788), the **Hippodrome** (021-622 7486) and the **Civic** and **Wulfrun Halls** in central Wolverhampton (0902-312030). The **XXXX** cabaret puts on up-and-coming Friday Night Live wannabees. On Wednesdays this is at the **Bear Tavern** in Bearwood Road, Bearwood (021-429 1184), and on Thursdays at the **Hare and Hounds** in King's Heath High Street (021-444 2081) and the **Billesley** in Brook Lane, Kings Heath (021-444 2357). A new XXXX Wednesday venue has recently opened in the Black Country at the **Cleveland Arms**, Stow Heath Lane in Wolverhampton. Tickets on the door or in advance for all four XXXX venues from the Birmingham Rep on 021-236 4455.

CINEMA

Mainstream Cinema

The places to go for a fine menu of Rambo XIIs and Police Academy 57s are as follows. Number of screens in square brackets.

- Odeon, New Street, Birmingham (021-643 6101). (6)
- Capitol Film Centre, Alum Rock Road, East Birmingham (021-327 0528). (3)
- Futurist Cannon, John Bright Street, Birmingham (021-643 0292). (2)
- King's Cinema, King's Square, West Bromwich (021-553 0192). (3)
- Cannon, Hagley Road West, Quinton, near Halesowen (021-422 2562). (4)
- Cannon, Townend Bank, Walsall (0922-22444). (3)
- Showcase, Bentley Mill Way, Walsall (0922-22123/22120). (12)
- UCI, Stratford Road, Monkspath, Solihull (021-733 3600/3636). (9)
- UCI, Merry Hill Centre (0384-78282). (10)
- Odeon, Maney Corner, Sutton Coldfield (021-354 2714). (4)
- Odeon, Castle Hill, Dudley (0384-55518). (2)
- Cannon, Garrick Street, Wolverhampton (0902-22917). (5)
- Warwick Cinema, Westley Road, Acock's Green (021-706 0766). (2)

Independent Cinema

There are some fine cinema experiences to be had in the region, although by no means as many as you would expect in a region of two million people.

In inner Birmingham, the Aston **Triangle** on Holt Street (buses 14, 43, 55, 93/4, 103/4) presents a varied diet of non-mainstream films, including matinées, late-night shows and theme seasons. It's not, however, the comfiest cinema in the world, always seeming to have an annoying draught whistling through it – and you (021-359 3979/4192).

MAC (née the Midlands Arts Centre) in Cannon Hill Park has a good range of mainstream and slightly more unusual films on at its two screens (021-440 3838/4221), as has the **Light House** media centre behind the Art Gallery in Lichfield Street, Wolverhampton (0902-312033). The two venues, plus the occasional screenings at the **Wide Angle** in Jenkins Street, Small Heath (021-772 2889), co-ordinate their avant-garde and unusual films together.

As you can see, the selection is a little thin. It's a bit like buses: you wait ages for some decent regular cinema and then fifteen events come at once – here during the annual **International Birmingham Film & TV Festival** in late September/early October. The Festival office is at The Bond, 180-182 Fazeley Street, Digbeth B5 5SE (021-766 6787). It has grown enormously in recent years, and there are many premières and excellent films on offer. Get your fill in during this fortnight – it's got to last you through a cold, lonely winter.

6. THE SHIRES OF MIDDLE ENGLAND: THE SURROUNDING AREAS

Luckily for Midlanders, with the exception of those living in Stratford or near Warwick Castle, the ravages of coach parties and thousands of gawping treasure-hunters have not really afflicted the region. This is not from a lack of things to see or appreciate: more a lack of awareness or inability to take a chance.

In fact – and to many people's surprise – the region around the urban areas of Birmingham and the Black Country is stunning; a patchwork of semi-rural England, dotted with (sometimes) interesting towns, (often) lovely villages and (nearly always) fabulous countryside. This section is split into three areas: **South-West and West**, covering Shropshire, Worcestershire and the southern finger of Staffordshire, **South-East and East**, covering Warwickshire, and **North**, covering the southern tip of Derbyshire and the rest of Staffordshire.

Each section is divided into areas, which are placed in a rough geographical order. Information on these areas cannot be exhaustive, and visitors are recommended to telephone or visit the local Tourist Information Centre. Further details of accommodation can be found in guides such as the excellent *BHRCA Hotels and Restaurants of Great Britain.*

To the South-west and West of the City

Without a doubt, this region – between Birmingham and Wales – is among the loveliest and least 'discovered' parts of Britain, well worth the effort of exploration. The pattern here is one of rolling hills, growing ever higher as they reach towards the Welsh border. Many of the smaller towns and villages well off the beaten track have avoided the stampede towards making the whole country one big commuter belt, although with improving roads, this is increasingly under threat. Nonetheless, the farther from the city and the nearer to Wales that you go, the easier it is to find Shropshire and Herefordshire life at a pace long since vanished from the streets of other so-called rural retreats.

TELFORD, THE WREKIN, IRONBRIDGE AND SHREWSBURY

- **Access:** ***Car*** – M6 and M54, B4176 or A458 and A442.
Rail – trains from New St and stations to Wolverhampton to Telford Central, Oakengates or Wellington Telford West. Bus service from Telford town centre to Ironbridge. Very occasional special trains run thorugh on the old line to Ironbridge.
Bus – Midland Red West express X60 and X61 from Wolverhampton to Telford and Ironbridge. Details of these and others on 0345-212555.
- **Tourist Information:** The Wharfage, **Ironbridge**; 0952-452204.
Telford Shopping Centre; 0952-291370 or 291723 for accommodation.
The Guildhall, Barrow Street, **Much Wenlock**; 0952-727679. (Summer only)
9 St Mary's Street, **Newport**; 0952-814109.
The Square, **Shrewsbury**; 0743-50761 or 50762 for accommodation.

The new town of Telford may not seem like the ideal weekend break, unless you are morbidly fascinated by the architecture of *Brookside* or in love with roundabouts. However, the good planners of the 1950s were not stupid in plonking Telford in the middle of a beautiful part of the world.

Most notable in the vicinity is the scourge of all school parties for the past thirty years, the **Ironbridge Gorge Museum**. If you last visited Ironbridge as a spotty, hormonally confused fourth-former, try and dispel the memories and take it in afresh. The gorge has remained largely undeveloped (barring chintzy tea shops) since the Victorian age, in great contrast to its neighbour, thirty-year-old Telford.

The iron bridge itself that spans the river Severn was built in 1779, the first of its kind in the world. The valley had been a centre of iron-smelting since Abraham Darby shouted 'Eureka!' on his production of cheap cast iron, seventy years earlier. The Ironbridge Gorge and Coalbrookdale became a veritable furnace of smelting activity, earning its role as the birthplace of the Industrial Revolution.

There is a great deal more to do here than just gawp at a bridge. The museum covers six sites, including the heritage township of the **Blists**

Hill Open Air Museum, the **Museum of the River** (including a fascinating 40-foot model of the Gorge in 1796), the **Museum of Iron**, the **Teddy Bear Shop & Museum** and the **Coalport China Museum**.

Some of the sites close during the winter – during British Summer Time, they are all open 1000-1800 daily. Wheelchair access is varied. Special events, such as theatre, exhibitions, regattas on the river and a Bonfire Night happen throughout the year. For details of all these aspects (and prices), contact the Visitor Information Service, Ironbridge Gorge Museum, Telford 0952-433522 (weekdays) or 2751/2166 (weekends).

Telford town centre is notable for its vast shopping centre and its ice rink (0952-291511). Beyond that, you should really head out of the town, which can be quite a challenge of navigation and sign-following in itself. Just west of the town is the 1,335-foot high, ridge-backed hump known as **The Wrekin**, a good climb with wonderful views far over Wales, the Peak District and the Malvern Hills. The best access is from the Forest Glen Hotel on the road from Little Wenlock to Wellington.

Five miles south-west of Ironbridge is **Much Wenlock**, the kind of town that most American visitors think the whole country is like. It's a town made up of architecture of most styles and ages: from the ruins of the Norman **St Milburga's Priory** to Tudor and Georgian houses. The town's idiosyncratic claim to fame is its annual **Olympic Games**, held every summer, and predating its modern upstart sibling by nearly fifty years. Details on 0952-727615.

Farther out in this direction are **Shrewsbury**, the ancient county town of Shropshire (briefly renamed Salop, and changed back after regular guffaws in the European Parliament every time the county was mentioned. *Salope* is French for whore. Ho-hum). Shrewsbury has one of the twinkiest, half-timbered town centres (set in a loop of the river Severn) that you could ever want. There's a full complement of a castle, several churches, museums and an abbey. Every August sees the renowned Shrewbury **Flower Show**. It's a good base to explore a beautiful part of the world.

BRIDGNORTH, KIDDERMINSTER, WYRE FOREST & THE SEVERN VALLEY

■ **Access:** *Car* – A454 from Wolverhampton, A458 from Stourbridge to Bridgnorth. A449 from W'hampton or A456 from Birmingham to Kidderminster.

Rail – Severn Valley Railway to Bridgnorth from Kidderminster, which is on the line from Birmingham, Stourbridge and Cradley Heath.
Bus – 0345-212555. Many buses to Kidderminster and some to Bridgnorth.

- **Tourist Information:** The Library, Listley Street, **Bridgnorth**; 0746-763358.
  The Travellers Joy, 47 High Street, **Kinver**; 0384-872940.
  Severn Valley station, Comberton Hill, **Kidderminster**; 0562-829400 (Summer only).
  Load Street, **Bewdley**; 0299-404740.
  Castle Street, **Ludlow**; 0584-875053.

Mid-Shropshire and north Worcestershire is one of the most accessible areas for West Midlanders gasping for a breath of the old rural smog. **Bridgnorth** is a common bolt-hole, with plenty of classic sights to ooh and aah over: the leaning keep of the castle (more angled than the tower of Pisa), the cliff railway connecting the old High and newer Low Towns, the steam trains on the Severn Valley Railway and the beautiful domed church of St. Mary Magdalene. Just outside the town, on the A458 Stourbridge road, is the **Midland Motor Museum** (0746-761761 for details).

Out of the town there are plenty of beautiful villages, walks and pubs: along the river Severn are the lovely villages of **Hampton Loade** and **Arley**, both bustling on a good summer's day with boozing Brummies taking a break from the steam railway. A good walk from Arley down the east bank of the river takes you to **Trimpley Reservoir** and the edges of the **Wyre Forest**.

Just a few miles west of Stourbridge lies the large village of **Kinver**, best known for the spectacular sandstone caves and park of **Kinver Edge**, but also well worth getting to know for its overwhelming collection of good pubs and restaurants. There are also some excellent regular book fairs in the village. Details on 021-550 0309. Bus 257 from Stourbridge or 584/588 from Wolverhampton and Kidderminster go to Kinver. The latter two buses also go to **Halfpenny Green Airport**, near Bobbington, home of a huge Sunday market.

Kidderminster (or Kiddy, as it's semi-affectionately known) is an industrial and market town that would seem more at home in Lancashire than in leafy Worcestershire. Its world-renowned carpet industry has waned, although some of the remaining factories have tours and shops (see *Shopping* in *SPORT AND LEISURE*). The town's college is the only place in Western Europe where you can do a degree in Carpet Studies! There are several very good pubs in the town: at the **Severn Valley Railway's** southern terminus station on Comberton Hill (next to the BR station) lies the **King and Castle**, a one-room, real-fire, real ale mecca. One of the jewels in 'Mad' O'Rourke's Little Pub Company crown is the **Little Tumbling Sailor** in Mill Street, complete with England's only inland lighthouse.

Four miles down the road from Kidderminster lies the town of **Stourport-on-Severn**, where the Staffordshire and Worcestershire Canal meets the river and which is, indeed, the only British town to exist as a result of the canal boom of the eighteenth century. Stourport has grand delusions of being Scarborough – in summer the main street is full of beachwear shops, chippies, amusement arcades, lads swilling lager and slapping on the sun cream. Instead of golden sands, Stourport has the river Severn and a few mudbanks, next to which are a couple of fun fairs that may prove to be a bit of let-down if you've ever been to Disneyland, but which can be good for a giggle. Lots of buses go to Stourport from Kidderminster.

Beyond Stourport on the A451 are **Great Witley** and the **Abberley Hills**. **Witley Court** is now but a ghostly shell of what was once one of the largest and most opulent stately homes in Britain. After a fire in the 1930s, decay gradually set in – but it is even more impressive because of it. The only part of the huge house that is untouched is the magnificent Baroque church, which contains a wall exhibition of the history of the Court.

Three miles west of Kidderminster lies the third town in Wyre Forest district: **Bewdley**. After downtrodden Kiddy and brash Stourport, Bewdley comes as a rather sedate, elegant shock. It's a beautiful Georgian riverside town that's gradually losing itself in a wash of twee tea shops, but which still has enough to entertain. The **Museum** in Load Street is excellent. The first Little Pub – **The Packhorse** – is in the High Street (which is not, confusingly, the main street). Midland Red buses X92 and 292 go from Birmingham and Halesowen through Kidderminster to Bewdley.

Between Kidderminster and Bewdley on the A456 lies the **West Midland Safari and Leisure Park**, a heady mix of wild animals, baboons showing their bottoms and stomach-churning land- and water-based rides. Avoid on a bank holiday.... Details on 0299-402114.

The A456 and A4117 snake west from Bewdley out towards **Ludlow** and the Welsh/English borderland, the **Marches**. Here are endless beautiful and quiet roads, remote villages and glorious walks. Buses X92 and 292 go from Birmingham out on the road to Ludlow, while others go from Kidderminster to the ancient town of **Tenbury Wells**, nestling in the sleepy Teme valley.

Just west of Bewdley lies the ancient **Wyre Forest**, offering many spectacular walks. Main access from the A456 at Callow Hill, two miles from Bewdley, or the B4194 Bewdley – Bridgnorth road. Places of note are far too plentiful to cover exhaustively here – some good village bases for walks (with excellent pubs to stagger back to) include **Hopton Wafers**, **Ditton Priors** and **Burwarton** (all around the Clee Hills); **Neen Sollars**, **Mamble**, **Bayton** and the beautiful small town of **Cleobury Mortimer** (all situated in pastoral orchard land surrounding the Teme valley).

Ludlow is one of the ancient border towns dominated by its huge **castle**, from which Edward I fought many battles against the tenacious Welsh. The castle particularly comes into its own during the annual early-summer **Ludlow Festival**, when it becomes the setting for excellent and atmospheric plays (one Shakespeare and one other) and concerts. Information on 0584-872150.

WORCESTER, THE MALVERNS AND THE VALE OF EVESHAM

■ **Access:**

Car – M5 to Worcester and thence to Malvern. A435 from Birmingham to Redditch and Evesham.
Rail – Regular services from New Street to Bromsgrove, Droitwich, Redditch, Worcester and Malvern. Trains from Worcester to Pershore and Evesham.
Bus – from Birmingham, Midland Red services to Worcester: X43 (also to Malvern), X44, X93, X94, 142, 144.

■ **Tourist Information:**

The Guildhall, High Street, **Worcester**; 0905-726311.
St Richard's House, Victoria Square, **Droitwich**; 0905-774312.
47-49 Worcester Road, **Bromsgrove**; 0527-31809.
Civic Square, Alcester Street, **Redditch**; 0527-60806.
Winter Gardens, Grange Road, **Malvern**; 0684-892289.
19 High Street, **Pershore**; 0386-554262.

Almonry Museum, Abbey Gate, **Evesham**; 0386-446944.

Lush valleys, ancient cathedrals and abbeys, rolling orchards, cider, plump and ruddy-faced yokel locals – these are things that the tourist board will have you believe abound in the southern half of Worcestershire and its tranquil twin, Herefordshire.

There's a lot of all that – but don't forget to watch out for the agro-industrial pesticides sprayed on those crunchy apples and the bits of church dropping off through recent decades of air pollution.

Nearer the West Midlands are the towns of Bromsgrove, Droitwich and Redditch. The latter two are largely Birmingham overspill towns (Redditch a designated new town), with acres of lego housing and disenchanted teenagers that seem to be linked inexorably with such a status. **Redditch** has the vast covered **Kingfisher Shopping Centre** at its heart, which provides the usual crop of chainstores, malls, fountains with Special Brew cans floating in them and bawling kids. **Droitwich** is an ancient spa town, with a new (and expensive) Brine Baths among its few half-timbered buildings and out-of-town furniture stores. **Bromsgrove** is a largely unremarkable town that has the **Avoncroft Museum of Buildings** on its outskirts. There are over twenty reconstructed buildings that you can wander around, spanning from the fourteenth-century Guesten Hall roof to a 1946 prefab. Attractions in between include a working windmill, an eighteenth-century earth closet and a cockpit theatre. Especially good for children. Open from the beginning of March until the end of November. Ring for times. Adults £2.30, children £1.15 at time of writing. Details from Avoncroft, Stoke Heath, Bromsgrove B60 4JR (0527-31886/31363). Bus 144 from Birmingham or Worcester.

The city of **Worcester** is overshadowed by the huge bulk of its beautiful cathedral, which contains the tomb of England's most unpopular monarch, King John. The cathedral is set in an idyllic position, next to the river Severn (the classic view from the Worcestershire County Cricket Ground over the river to the cathedral has adorned many 'Beautiful Olde England' coffee-table books). One of the most peaceful walks is along the towpath from the river bridge down to the cathedral.

There is plenty to see and do in Worcester, which has succeeded in not sacrificing all its reality to chintzy teashops. Yet. Museums include the **Commandery Civil War Centre** in Sidbury, recalling the battle of Worcester, which was the last major skirmish in the English Civil War. The

Commandery is a fifteenth-century building that served as the Royalist headquarters. Also of note is the **Tudor House** museum in Friar Street.

There are plenty of small back streets and alleys in the city, many of which house interesting shops and non-touristy pubs. Some of the better drinking haunts include the **Cardinal's Hat** in Friar Street, near the cathedral, the **Lamb & Flag** in the Tything, serving excellent beer, and the Jolly Roger ale home-brew pub, the **Brewery Tap** in Lowesmoor. Worcester plays host to the **Three Choirs Festival** every third summer (1993/6/9), alternating with Hereford and Gloucester. This covers all kinds of classical and choral music, including much by Worcester's very own **Edward Elgar**.

About seven miles south-west of Worcester lie the **Malvern** towns, renowned for their spa waters, clear air, elegant surroundings and genteel streets clinging to the edge of the **Malvern Hills**. The hills make for excellent and leisurely walking, with spectacular views over Herefordshire and the Vale of Evesham. Access to the more popular Worcestershire Beacon from Great Malvern town (and station), the quieter southern end from Colwall station or the A449 at Wynds Point. There are some excellent pubs and slightly twee restaurants in Malvern: noteworthy are the **Royal Malvern** in Graham Road for good vegetarian food and the excellent **Railway** pub in Wells Road, Malvern Wells.

To the east of Worcester lies the verdant **Vale of Evesham**, stretching down to the edge of the Cotswold Hills. The Vale is a notable centre of market gardening watered by the river Avon, dotted with pretty villages with slightly odd names (Upton Snodsbury, Drakes Broughton and Wyre Piddle for instance). The small town of **Pershore** is renowned for its **abbey**. Just to the south of Pershore lies the smooth round hump of **Bredon Hill**, around which are some pretty villages and excellent country pubs: in **Elmley Castle**, the **Combertons** and **Eckington**. Sadly, much of the area seems to have been bought up by BMW drivers who shoot around the lanes and curse tractors or herds of cows that dare get in their God-given way, but it is still worth exploring. Pick of the pubs is the **Anchor** in Wyre Piddle, which somehow provides a real atmosphere of rural retreat, in the middle of some fabulous countryside.

Evesham itself is a pleasant market town on the banks of the river Avon. There are some pleasant strolls and a few good town centre pubs, many serving the comparatively local brew, Hook Norton. An excellent Hookie pub nearby is the thatched **Fleece Inn** in the neighbouring village of **Bretforton**.

To the South-east and East of the City

This region is more accessible for those wanting a little country cottage to commute to, and as a result suffers from a lack of native identity in parts.

STRATFORD, WARWICK & LEAMINGTON

- **Access:** *Car* – M40 to Warwick (or old A41), old A34 to Stratford.
  Rail – trains from Birmingham to Stratford and to Warwick and Leamington. Also from Leamington and Warwick to Stratford.
- **Tourist Information:** Judith Shakespeare's House, 1 High Street, **Stratford-upon-Avon**; 0789-293127.
  The Court House, Jury Street, **Warwick**; 0926-492212
  Royal Pump Room, The Parade, **Leamington Spa**; 0926-311470.

For those with just 48 hours in Britain, Stratford is probably already on your list. If you're very lucky, you might get half-an-hour at Warwick Castle while you're in the area. This part of England is mercilessly exploited for its tourist charms, while many of its hidden secrets remain well away from Elmer Jr. and Veronica's ruthless stare.

Stratford is all that you feared, and more. Every Shakespeare connection is ruthlessly and ritually murdered, to the extent where the real town and its history become almost submerged in a sea of commercialism. Most importantly, there is the **Royal Shakespeare Company** and its three auditoria: the **main theatre**, housing a steady but pricey diet of well-produced Bill the Shakes productions with glittering casts; the **Swan Theatre**, a fairly recent innovation that aims to put on You Know Who's lesser-known works, as well as many by his fellow Jacobean and Elizabethan writers and the **Other Place**, a corrugated shack that houses all strands and styles of theatre and dramatic discussions. Details on 0789-295623.

Then, of course, there is a veritable Pandora's Box of tenuous links with the Bard: the **Shakespeare Centre** next to the **Birthplace Museum**; WS's later house (long since demolished but the garden's still there) – **New Place**; his wife **Anne Hathaway's Cottage** in Shottery and his old ma's (**Mary Arden)** bijou little pad in nearby Wilmcote; and his burial place in the river-side **Holy Trinity Church**. There's also a wonderful range of nasty little tea rooms, gift shops and tourist-trap pubs with crass names like Illyria, As You Like It, Elsinore and The Merry Wives. Some of the better alehouses in Shakespeareland are the **Old Tramway** on the Shipston Road and the **White Swan** in Rother Street, an orgy of oak panelling and none-too-cheap food. Celeb spotters always head for the haunt of many a frustrated and booming-voiced thesp, the rather expensive **Dirty Duck**, next to the RSC Theatre in Waterside, or the **Garrick** in the High Street.

Around Stratford, there are some beautiful villages well worth exploring: **Charlecote**, with its Hall and Deer Park where guess who was said to have poached in his wild early days; nearby **Hampton Lucy** and **Alveston**, with its excellent riverside pub, the **Ferry**. Downstream from Stratford is the straggling village of **Wellford-on-Avon** – try the **Bell** in the High Street.

The well-worn coach trail then moves inexorably to **Warwick**, chiefly to gaze in awe at the magnificent **castle**, bought up a few years ago by Madame Tussaud's, which should explain the proliferation of rather sallow wax figures in period dress around the place. The castle **rose garden** is magnificent. Open from 1000 every day (until 1730 in summer, 1630 in winter). Details on 0926-495421.

Warwick has a beautiful, if fairly unexciting, town centre. More stimulating for a shopping frenzy is neighbouring **Leamington** (or, more formally, Royal Leamington Spa), a pleasant, Regency town that comprises wide avenues, graceful architecture and beautiful parks and gardens. And a lot of shops. Of great reputation is the UK's first **Levi's shop** on The Parade, stocking the whole range of hip denim wear, tops and chinos. Behind is the **Royal Priors** shopping centre, in which you need an engineering or maths degree to understand the natty Peacock clock.

The **Jephson Gardens** at the bottom of the Parade are worth taking your bag of crumbs to for the ducks, while the nearby **Royal Spa Centre** (0926-334418) is a regular venue for wrestling and semi-famous MOR performers in pastel pullovers.

The local countryside is pleasantly rolling, without being breathtaking: many local villages offer pleasant and very relaxed meandering – **Barford**, the birthplace and home of Joseph Arch, who orchestrated the formation of agricultural trade unions from a public meeting held under a chestnut tree in nearby **Wellesbourne**, going on to become a national figure and Liberal MP. The old Red Lion pub has been renamed the Joseph Arch, and there is an impressive obelisk of

Cornish granite on his grave in the village church yard. On the other side of the Avon from Barford lies the hamlet of **Sherbourne**, with its beautiful and serene church.

To the east of Leamington runs the ruler-straight Roman Road, the **Fosse Way**, which is worth basing yourself upon to explore some of the local countryside. Worthwhile areas include the thatch and half-timber village of **Offchurch**, with interesting local walks along the river Leam and the sleepily rural Grand Union Canal. The **Stag's Head** pub in Offchurch is deservedly known for the quality – and variety – of its food. Farther down the Fosse Way lies the tiny but elongated village of **Chesterton**, with its remote windmill, ponds and ancient church at the end of the tiny track.

Other villages worth passing time in include **Moreton Morrell**, **Combrook** (especially for the woods and lakeland of nearby Compton Verney) and **Kineton**.

COVENTRY AND NORTH WARWICKSHIRE

■ **Access:** *Car* – A45 or M6 Birmingham to Coventry. M6 also to Nuneaton and M6/M69 to Hinckley and Leicester. A45 and A452 to Kenilworth.
Rail – Trains from New Street and Birmingham International to Coventry, and New Street to Nuneaton, Hinckley and Leicester. Bus from Coventry to Kenilworth.

■ **Tourist Information:** Central Library, Smithford Way, **Coventry**; 0203-832312.
Library, 11 Smalley Place, **Kenilworth**; 0926-52595/50708.
Library, Church Street, **Nuneaton**; 0203-384027 or 347006 for accommodation.
Library, Lancaster Road, **Hinckley**; 0455-30852.
Bosworth Battlefield, near **Sutton Cheney**; 0455-292239. Summer only.

This region is regularly overlooked as containing anything of great interest. In fact, while there are undoubtedly drab parts, it is characterized by winding lanes, woods, hills and sleepy (if sometimes over-commuterized) villages with very old English names.

The city of **Coventry** has risen to prominence since the Second

World War, largely due to the extensive rebuilding necessary after the blitz that obliterated whole swathes of the city. Before the war, Coventry was an unremarkable industrial Midlands city, with a parish church lately upgraded to the status of cathedral. Thousands of people worked in the dominant motor industry.

Sir Basil Spence's remarkable new **cathedral** focused the international eye on the city. Lying next to the bombed-out ruins of the old cathedral, the vast bulk contains mesmerizing stained glass and is dominated by the massive Sutherland tapestry of Christ. The ruins of the old cathedral provide a dramatic setting for the annual Coventry **Mystery Plays** (0203-553055). Nearby, in Jordan Well, is the **Herbert Museum and Art Gallery** (open daily), which includes an interesting exhibition of the city's history.

One of Coventry's best-known claims to fame is as the historic home of **Lady Godiva**, whose nude ride through the town in protest against her husband's taxes could provide a more interesting role model for latter-day poll-tax demonstrations. A statue (with a suitably cheekie chappie Peeping Tom clock) commemorating the event is in Broadgate.

After the blitz, the city centre was totally replanned in the immediate post-war years. Sadly, the concept of open, pedestrianized shopping walkways of the 1950s became windy, desolate and dingy precincts of the 1970s and 1980s. Much effort has been made to clear 'undesirable elements' off the streets, including the nationwide pilot scheme to ban drinking in public open spaces. With the decline in manufacturing industries in the early eighties, increasing numbers of people (especially young people) had little more to do than to hang around the pedestrianized city centre. During this time, Coventry briefly became the centre of the British music scene in churning out ska and two-tone music from groups such as the Specials, The Selecter and the Bodysnatchers (who metamorphosed into the Belle Stars). The music reflected the Midlands mood: cynical, disenchanted and fighting for multi-racial acceptability. Perhaps the greatest moment came when The Specials' deeply contemptuous *Ghost Town* topped the charts at the time of Chuck and Di's 1981 wedding.

Much of the youth culture that came into being in the early 1980s has been honed into a more sophisticated brand for the new decade. Most impressive is the multi-use **Tic Toc Club**, in Primrose Hill Street (0203-632462). Theatre, comedy, cabaret, dance, live music and drinking all combine in this excellent and animated venue. The city's **Belgrade Theatre**, in Corporation Street (0203-553005), has occasional flashes of brilliance in among the rather more turgid family productions and minor TV celebs. Four miles from the city centre is the highly successful and very imaginative **University of Warwick Arts Centre**, which plays host to a staggering repertoire of travelling theatre, dance, music and comedy companies, as well as having a cinema showing good arts and classic films not generally being shown in the Odeon or Cannon chains. One of the problems is that it is very difficult to get to if you don't have a car, as the occasional No.12 bus to the University winds its way around the housing estates of Stivichall and Canley. Box office and details on 0203-524524. Tickets also available at the Birmingham Ticket Shop in City Arcade (021-643 2514).

Pubs in the city centre tend to be in the marginally unexciting vein; most serving endless frothy streams of keg M&B or Ansells. The **Rising Sun** in spruced-up Spon Street is friendly and popular. A large jazz pub in the busy suburb of Earlsdon, the **Earlsdon Cottage** (Warwick Street) is busy and worth a visit.

A few miles south of Coventry lies the **National Agricultural Centre** at Stoneleigh (avoid local roads during big events such as the Royal Show), and the small town of **Kenilworth**. The ancient and enormous sandstone **castle** with its chequered and often bleak history is the town's best-known attraction. Beyond that, there is a compact and standard town centre, with some pleasant pubs: on the main street, Warwick Road, the **Earl Clarendon**, in New Street, the **Royal Oak** and up near the castle on Castle Hill, the **Clarendon Arms**. The multi-roomed and very good **Virgins and Castle** is in the High Street – which is most certainly not the main street! The nearby village of **Ashow** is lovely for wooded and riverside walking.

To the north-west of Coventry, in the hinterland between the city and the West Midlands conurbation, there is some agreeable countryside dotted with ancient stately homes, villages that have sadly suffered for their prettiness and close proximity to major cities, some undulating, remote lanes, hills, farms and woods. Worth exploring are the areas around **Coleshill**, an ancient coaching town (try the very good **George & Dragon** in the High Street), the nearby **Shustoke Reservoirs** (don't miss the wonderful **Griffin** pub in Shustoke village), **Nether** and **Old Whitacre**, **Old Arley** and **Fillongley** (the nearby village of **Corley Moor** has the peaceful old village pub, the **Bull & Butcher**, to discover).

North of Coventry lies the town of **Bedworth**, and beyond that, the neighbouring towns of **Nuneaton** and **Hinckley**, divided by the A5 (the Roman Watling Street) and the Warwickshire/Leicestershire border.

Right off the beaten track to the east of Bedworth is the hamlet of **Barnacle**, containing one of the best, and totally genuine, country pubs – the **Red Lion** – in the area.

Nuneaton clings to its famous daughter, George Eliot – the name appears everywhere, although it certainly hasn't succeeded in turning the town into a second Stratford. Phew. A couple of miles to the south-west of Nuneaton is **Arbury Hall**, where Eliot (then known as Mary Ann Evans) was born in a farmhouse on the estate . The Hall is open to public, and is well worth the effort. It's a phantasmagoric Elizabethan manor that was gothicized a few centuries later, and now lies in a spectacular lakeside setting. Good walking is also on the cards around the village of **Hartshill** and the **Hartshill Hayes Country Park**, two miles north-west of Nuneaton.

Five miles north of Hinckley is **Bosworth Field**, where the final battle of the Wars of the Roses was fought in 1485. Today's battle is making your way around the visitor centre, cafeteria and associated fripperies, although walking down by the Ashby-de-la-Zouch Canal, Ambion Wood and the grounds of Shenton Hall can be very pleasant. The small town of **Market Bosworth**, a couple of miles up the road, is worth seeing.

To the North of the City

STAFFORDSHIRE

- **Access:** ***Car*** – M6 to Cannock and Stafford. A38 to Burton and Lichfield.
  Rail – Services from New Street to Lichfield City, Stafford, Hednesford, Tamworth and Burton-on-Trent. Trains from Stafford to Rugeley and Lichfield Trent Valley.
- **Tourist Information:** Marmion House, Lichfield Street, **Tamworth**; 0827-311222.
  Town Hall, King Edward Place, **Burton-on-Trent**; 0283-5454..
  Prince of Wales Centre, Church Street, **Cannock**; 0543-66453.
  The Old Library, **Lichfield**; 0543 252109.
  The Ancient High House, Greengate Street, **Stafford**; 0785-0204.

The bulk of the country north of Birmingham and the Black Country forms the county of Staffordshire, which used to contain most of the grimiest parts of the Black Country. Since local government reorganization, Staffordshire has become a pleasantly rural county of small towns, forests, rivers and hills surrounding the scars of the mining industry. There is a great deal more to the county of Staffordshire than Alton Towers, the UK's nearest answer to Disneyworld. Like many of its Midland neighbours, it is a much underrated county that warrants considerable exploration.

At the eastward edge are the towns of **Tamworth** and **Burton-on-Trent**. Tamworth's ancient castle and beautiful parish church of St. Editha are the town's most obvious attractions, although the surrounding countryside is worthy of some perusal. Just to the south is the very popular **Drayton Manor Park**, packed to the gunwales with attractions, a zoo, fairground rides and some very attractive plastic dinosaurs. Most kids may well get the impression that the *Tyrannosaurus rex* had 'West Brom rule' etched indelibly on its leg. Further details on 0827-87979. The park is next to the village of **Fazeley**, at the end of the eminently walkable **Birmingham and Fazeley Canal**.

Burton-on-Trent is an industrial town that seems to owe more to the North than the English Midlands. But don't pass it by, for its staple industry is brewing. A sticky smell of hops and yeast hangs over the town. The **Bass Museum of Brewing** (including the stables of the Bass shire horses) is a comprehensive study of brewing methods ancient and modern, complete with reconstructions of nineteenth-century offices and laboratories and A/V displays. The reconstructed Edwardian pub gives you the chance to have a go at the traditional pub games and to sup from old vessels. The museum is open daily until 1700 (from 1000 Monday-Friday, 1030 Saturday and Sunday). Location: Horninglow Street (A50) (0283-45301 weekdays, 42031 weekends). There is also the rather blandly named **Heritage Brewery Museum** on Anglesey Road. Details on 0283-69226.

In a town that produces lakes of ale every day, putting a pint or two of it down your throat comes quite easy. The **Bridge Brewery** in Bridge Street can be visited, and has an excellent frontispiece pub. Marstons Pedigree is one of the better Burton brews, and it's available on the home patch at the **Black Horse** in Moor Street and the **Derby Inn** on Derby Road among many others. Not that you're ever very far from a pub in Burton – if desperate, you could always just sniff the air!

Ten miles down the A38 from Burton is the small city of **Lichfield**, with the three spires of its impressive **cathedral** visible for miles around.

Beyond that, the city is the birthplace of the Jonathan Miller of the eighteenth century, Dr Samuel Johnson, whose birthplace in Breadmarket Street is now, needless to say, a museum (0543-264972). Drink at the excellent **Queens Head** in Queen Street.

A few miles north of the city is the pretty village of **Hamstall Ridware**, most notable for its **Arts Centre** in the ancient manor house. Very good for arty-crafty items and wholemeal lifestyles in a rural setting. Check times of opening on 088922-351.

Other villages and areas in eastern Staffordshire that warrant a visit include those within the boundaries of the historic **Needwood Forest**, to the west of Burton. Today, the Forest is only really a patchy series of seemingly unconnected, but nonetheless beautiful, woods interspersed with some pleasant villages, such as **Hoar Cross**, **Yoxall**, **Anslow** (try the marvellous **Bell** pub), **Rangemore** (complete with the beautiful grounds of the otherwise rather twee **Byrkley Park** garden and craft centre) and **Abbots Bromley** (near the impressive and large **Blithfield Reservoir** which can be crossed by causeway on the B5013). September in Abbots Bromley also sees the annual **Horn Dance**, a Monty Pythonesque Olde English Custom that makes morris dancing seem natural.

Cannock Chase forest and country park is only about ten miles north of Walsall. As a result, it is very much one of the favourite green play areas for the good folk of the West Midlands conurbation, and on a Sunday afternoon can resound to the sound of yapping family pooches and bawling lost kids. All the same, there is more than enough space for everyone, and you can usually wander far enough to lose yourself in the sylvan glades. Best places for access are from the A460 from Hednesford or any of the roads going to the west from Rugeley.

To the south of the Chase, on the way to Walsall, is the fun and free **Chasewater Leisure Park**, just off the A5 on the outskirts of Brownhills. There's a model railway, sailing, power-boating, lots of wildlife and children's play area all around the large reservoir. Information on 0543-452623.

Just to the north of the Chase is **Shugborough Hall** and **Park**, the ancestral home of camera-toting Lord Lichfield. The park plays host to mock battles, balloon rallies, a rare breeds farm and working mill. Open all year. Details on 0889-881388.

The county town of **Stafford** has a few things of traditional interest: a good **Art Gallery** in Lichfield Road (0785-57303), complete with extensive adjoining **Craft Shop** and a fair selection of half-timbered houses and dinky little streets. Renowned eighteenth-century wit and dramatist Richard Brinsley Sheridan was the town's MP.

Villages between Stafford and the northern tip of Wolverhampton offer a pleasant collection of canal and river-side walks. The village of **Brewood**, straddling the Shropshire Union canal, has some excellent pubs to sample: the Holt, Plant and Deakin **Admiral Rodney** in Dean Street, the **Swan** in The Square (complete with skittle alley) and the nearby **New Inns** on the road to Bishop's Wood at **Kiddemore Green**, a very pleasant rural location. Just to the south is the imposing **Chillington Hall**, which has some beautiful walks in the vicinity, including the wooded avenues that lead to the front door from the Shropshire Union canal, some two miles away.

And so to **Alton Towers**.... Although near Uttoxeter, in northern Staffordshire, and so pedantically out of range of this book, the place casts its net over the whole Midlands. Beautiful parkland, places to eat and drink, loads of rides to throw it up on afterwards – generally, *the* place for an expensive, but unforgettable, day out. Loads of bus companies operate regular tours to Alton Towers from Birmingham and the Black Country. Details on 0538-702200.

7. SPORT AND LEISURE

Shopping

In and around the West Midlands you can usually find just about any kind of shop that you may need – sometimes, however, you might just have to look quite hard. In common with most British towns, Midland town centres are gradually homogenizing into one identical format; the only variation being in the differential floor space of any one of the major chains.

BIRMINGHAM

The centre of the England's second city is compact and comprises a few unusual and interesting shops, as well as the predictable megastores that attack your nostrils with clouds of Chanel on entry. It's a hybrid of 1960s planning (if it could be described as planning), with gloomy walkways and urine-soaked underpasses brushing alongside striking Victorian buildings and modern shopping complexes (often designed to look like the self-same Victorian arcades). The Great God Motor Car ruled the minds of Birmingham's developers, leaving the befuddled pedestrian to scuttle and delve through the underpasses, popping up for air and daylight like a startled mole. Recent years have seen gathering momentum to humanize the city centre once again, and to turn the throttling Inner Ring Road back into a pedestrian-level street.

The city centre has not escaped without its fair clutch of brand-new 'climatically controlled total shopping experiences' (i.e. shopping centres), bearing such highly imaginative names as the Plaza, the Pavilions and the Pallasades. Hanging on in there is the infamous, very large, down-to-earth and much-maligned **Bull Ring** shopping centre, which lies cowering under the Rotunda. Together, they really represent people's perceptions of Brum: city of the sixties and seventies.

The future of the Bull Ring and the Rotunda is the subject of fierce current debate, as Those In Charge have finally woken up to the fact that people do not especially appreciate a swathe of concrete precinct where the city centre used to be. Plans to date for the area's future seem more encouraging. Next to the Bull Ring is the **Pallasades** – the tarted-up butterfly that emerged from the drab chrysalis that was catchily named the Birmingham Shopping Centre. It is into the Pallasades that you are first launched on any shopping frenzy, heading out of New Street station on the escalators.

Markets

Birmingham's 800-year-old markets are the city's shopping pride and joy. They range from very specialist groupings to dozens of smaller general household/clothes stalls that you will stumble across all over the city centre at the crossroads of various underpasses.

There is a vast permanent indoor market in the **Bull Ring**, selling most things from knickers to knick-knacks. It's open daily (except Sunday and Wednesday afternoon), and until 2000 on Thursday. It is particularly good for fresh food, fruit and vegetables, found both in the Market Hall and the open-air market. The hall is – surprisingly, perhaps – famous for its fresh fish.

Of greater interest is the **Rag Market**, and its neighbours, the **Row** and **Flea Markets**. These are open on Tuesday (best day for bargains), Friday and Saturday, and are situated in Edgbaston Street, just behind the Bull Ring. You can find bargains a-plenty at these markets, held in and around cavernous warehouses and street-corners. Clothes, materials, household and DIY, as well as food and semi-trendy bric-à-brac are the best buys here, as well as giving you the chance to indulge in the ancient arts of a good rummage and an even better barter. On Mondays from 0900-1400 the site plays host to the vast and avarice-inducing **Antiques Market**.

A recent city council initiative has been to sponsor a small **Ethnic Bazaar** in the Bull Ring open-air market. Here you can buy all manner of chic wall hangings, bangles and the like – essential for that housing co-op in Harborne that you're looking for.

Clothes Shopping

Beyond the markets and the muzak-toting chain stores, Birmingham has a fair variety of clothes shops. A few years ago, **Oasis** at 112 Corporation Street was the most exciting store in the city, consisting of a labyrinth of underground tunnels, stalls, a deadbeat café and record shop that all combined to provide hours of unhassled browsing and frequent rewards. Sadly, this is no longer the case, after someone's enlightened decision to smarten the place up and turn it into a sanitized version of Top Shop. It's still passable for some denim and leather goods, though its metamorphosis is a huge turn for the worse.

The fashion heritage trail peaks at the newly crowned Brum Centre of Trendiness: **Folio 50** (at 137 Digbeth and in the Piccadilly Arcade off New Street). They specialize in 1950s-inspired clothes and accessories. The Digbeth store also houses a café – *the* place, no doubt, to strut your 501s. In a similar nostalgic vein is the **Razor's Edge** at 83 Hurst Street.

Also in Piccadilly Arcade lies the **Depot**, a fair-priced menswear store that offers a collection of hip and vogue vestments aimed at perhaps a slightly more upwardly mobile clientele. Rather more downmarket, but lots more fun and decidedly cheaper, is a vast bargain store (mainly for women) in the Bull Ring named **Mark One**, where you can buy all those necessities at notoriously knock-down prices. **Alive** at 85, Bull Street and also in the Rotunda Subway sell a whole load of Army surplus gear for the more cosmopolitan members of the community, as well as the (fairly) latest in trendy teeshirts and tops – some of which, however, do seem to be overly preoccupied with British Bulldogs and the Union Jack.

A chic little enclave of high fashion is the parade of six shops on **Ethel Street**, a tiny road off New Street up towards the Town Hall. If you want – and can afford – to kit yourself out à la Pam Hogg, Katherine Hamnett, Junior Gaultier, E Ginelli – or even snap up a futon, this is the place. Not quite South Molton Street, but then again, it's certainly not the Bull Ring either. Ever so 1990s – and that's a good twenty years further on than most of the surrounding shops.

For the well-heeled guy or gal around town, **Next 2 Nothing** in Corporation Street provides a plethora of ex-Next catalogue stock at comparatively cut prices. They are particularly good for small sizes. **Reiss**, at 32a New Street, are also worth seeking out for someone of that ilk.

For those of a simple nature, there's a thumping great **Marks and Spencer** store in the High Street, interconnecting with the neighbouring **Pavilions** shopping centre. M&S is the undisputed champion of undies and ready-made bubble'n'squeak, while the Pavilions boasts that it was crowned with the 'European International Shopping Centre Award' for 1988. Just who on earth takes themselves so seriously to decree such a meaningless and utterly uninteresting laurel? Is it the same Euro-flunkies who decide that it's International Asparagus Day or the European Week of Indigenous Folk Dancing?

Inside the European Shopping Experience of the Millennium, you'll begin to understand just why it merits such a very important title. You will doubtless stand and be amazed by the variety of fascinating and hitherto unexplored emporia: Dorothy Perkins, Athena, Tie Rack, Dolcis, Principles, Next, Body Shop, the Suit Company. And there's more – but I'd hate to get you too excited.

The stonking great department stores of Birmingham present the shopper with some good stuff, especially for clothes. **Rackhams** in Temple Row is especially worth some serious perusal, and **Lewis's** in Bull Street can be worth a good elbow in the sales.

One of the results of Birmingham's diverse racial mix is that it is easy to buy beautifully made and colourful **ethnic clothes** and fabric. The best places for this are Edgbaston Street in the city centre, or – just out of the city centre – along the A45 Coventry Road in Small Heath, the A34 Stratford Road in Sparkbrook or the A41 Soho Road in Handsworth. A place to get remarkably cheap material to construct your own wonder piece is **International Stock** in Silver Street, King's Heath.

There are a few good **second-hand** clothes shops in **Hurst Street**, which comes off the Smallbrook Queensway, running by the markets and the Hippodrome. Here, as in any second-hand place, it pays to have a good ferret around. The rest of the city centre has a solid variety of all kinds of clothes shopping, especially in the smaller streets away from the Pallasades crowds.

Just a short bus ride away is **Moseley** (bus 35 from the Station Street garage, bus 50 from the bottom of New Street by the Rotunda, bus 1 from Five Ways to Acocks Green or Midland Red buses 177/8/9 to Redditch). Here you will find a fine selection of new, and especially second-hand, clothes shops on and around the Alcester Road. Of particular note for its eternally high status is **Houghtons** at 115 Alcester Road (021-449 9953), specializing in second-hand clothes from the 1920s to the sixties and seventies.

Harborne (buses 3, 11, 20/1/2/3/5/9, 448, 653) is a chic little enclave with some suitably twinky shops. In the High Street you will find the **Arcade Market**, daily from Tuesday to Saturday, which combines a fine blend of arty, crafty things with food and all those fripperies for the earnest *Guardian* reader.

Other good areas for second-hand hunting are a little farther afield, but worth the effort – try **Acock's Green** (Spring Road or Acock's Green station or buses 1, 11, 37, 44, 181), the very well-heeled **Solihull**, where only the best things are given to those charity shops (Solihull station or dozens of buses) and the neighbouring upmarket suburb of **Shirley** (buses 3, 4, 5, 6, 48/9, 69/A, 162, 190/1).

For **jumble sales**, look in the local free weeklies or the daily freebie, the *Birmingham Daily News*. For the best run-down of the weekend menu of Scout halls and draughty community centres, splash out on Friday's edition of the *Evening Mail* for Birmingham or the *Express & Star* for Wolverhampton and the Black Country.

Book Shopping

Birmingham is not blessed with the kind of speciality bookshops that you might perhaps expect in a city of its size. In the city centre there are two major book 'superstores': **Dillons** (formerly the much-loved Hudson's) on New Street and **Waterstone's** on the corner of New Street and High Street. Both offer a wide and plentiful stock with a good proportion of local books. Both are very large. Out of the national chains, these are probably the best two to have in town.

The omnipresent **W.H.Smith** has a large branch in central Brum (at 29 Union Street) that covers a huge range of mainstream titles. Near the top of the escalator from New Street station in the Pallasades is **Hornby's**: much smaller than its three big siblings, but with a very helpful and interested staff.

Key Books at 136 Digbeth (021-643 8081) is the city's most noted radical bookshop: from copies of papers, periodicals and magazines of the Left, anarchic and green wings of thought to books, teeshirts, badges and posters covering all areas of ideologically sound thinking. There is also a small right-on bookshop at the **MAC** in Cannon Hill Park. Both shops stock non-sexist, non-racist and generally good-egg children's books, as do **Positive Image** at Zair Works, 111-119 Bishop Street, Birmingham B5 6JL (021-622 5921).

Far more of a bourgeois deviation is **Her Majesty's Stationery Office (HMSO)**, which is especially good for maps, guides and local interest books, as well as the chance to get to grips with the more exciting details of the Sewers and Drains Reform Provision (Wales) Act. It is only open Monday-Friday, and is situated a little out of the shopping areas on Broad Street, almost opposite the International Convention Centre. And you can't be in Brum for five minutes without knowing where *that* is.

The shop on the first floor of the **Central Library** in Chamberlain Square/Paradise Place is excellent for a huge variety of local stuff. You can pick up local cycling leaflets and booklets, as well as some light-hearted West Midland writing. And, as if that wasn't enough, the shop has a comprehensive supply of those essential pressies or souvenirs – Brum tea-towels, Brum furry gonks, Brum rubbers (that's erasers for our Stateside cousins...) and, no doubt, guides to mastering the accent for those who want to stun their friends into appreciative silence.

A few 'bargain' ex-catalogue and discount bookshops pepper the city centre. Most obvious is **Booksale** in the High Street, opposite the Pavilions centre. If you search hard enough, you might even find a book that *isn't* about gardening, the Royals or astrology.

The best **second-hand** bookshop is out of the city centre at 567, Bristol Road in Selly Oak (buses 61/2/3 or Selly Oak station). This is the crisply named **Birmingham Book Shop**, and is within handy panicking distance of both Birmingham University and Westhill College. Smaller, but mustier and absolutely fascinating, is **Maxwell's** in Shaftmoor Lane, between Sparkhill and Acock's Green (near Spring Road station). In Harborne High Street, the eccentric **Blitzgeist Books** sells a load more besides (jewellery, clothes, videos), and all of a suspiciously hippy nature.

Record Shopping

HMV (New Street) and **Virgin** (98 Corporation Street) are the standard record megastores, replete with video screens and wall-to-wall Stock, Aitken and Waterman.

Beyond these, there is a veritable mecca for jazz and swing specialists at 45, Loveday Street, beyond the Inner Ring Road at the top of Corporation Street: the imaginatively named **Record Centre** (021-359 7399). Aficionados come from all over Britain to this shop, which provides a real sanctuary from Sonia and Big Fun. Try also the **Plastic Factory** at 189 Corporation Street (021-233 2967), **Swordfish** in Needless Alley, **Second City Sounds** at 57 Summer Row (021-236 8648), **Tempest** at 83 Bull Street (021-236 9170) or **Frank's Wild Records**, at 19 St Martin's House in the Bull Ring (021-643 0967) for a wider selection of less mainstream new and second-hand rock tracks.

For a selection of reggae, soul, rap and house, try **Don Christie's** at 10-12 Gloucester Street in the city centre, (021-622 5420), or **Summit** at 44-45 Bull Ring in Birmingham (021-643 7895) and 7A Cleveland Street, Wolverhampton.

Rare Treats

Somewhat few and far between, I'm afraid, but don't give up trying....
Pottery and Pieces – despite its slightly dinky name – is one of the best and most interesting gift and unusual jewellery shops in the city. However, you'll have to hop on a bus (for numbers see above), as

they're in Moseley – at the rear of St Mary's Row in Moseley centre (021-449 7915).

On a more ethereal plane, **Turtles** at 498, Bristol Road in Selly Oak (021-471 2301), will flog you food, flowery clothes, books, ornaments, cards, jewellery and household gear of a mystical air, guaranteed to keep your joss-stick of life alight. Just down the road, at 550 Bristol Road, **Inti** is an unusual Latin American art and craft shop (021-472 3983), just perfect for the Christmas present for that awkward auntie.... For directions, see Birmingham Book Shop above. In a slightly similar vein, the **One Earth Shop** at Friends of the Earth, 54 Allison Street, Digbeth (021-632 6909), has a comprehensive supply of herbal remedies, wholefood, organic veg, books, cycling packs and readymix beards.

Nostalgia and Comics at 14-16, Smallbrook Queensway (021-643 0143), city centre, has a vast supply of (not surprisingly) comics, as well as mementoes from TV and film.

For the true movie buff, the **Cinema Shop** at 45 Summer Row, near the Paradise Circus Queensway, stocks a huge range of memorabilia and publications. It is supposed to be open every afternoon from Tuesday until Saturday, although this can't always be depended on.... Probably best to ring first on 021-236 9879.

Food Shopping

For most of your everyday needs, the markets in central Brum (or any of the other towns in the region) will keep you stocked with a ready supply of fresh and pretty cheap fruit and veg, meat, fish and dairy produce. The Bull Ring is especially good for this. For more specific needs, the city centre does have some good foodie places to discover. For unusual **Chinese** delicacies, **Jason Hong Supermarket** in the Bull Ring Centre going down towards Digbeth is a great source of inspiration. A little farther down, behind Digbeth High Street in Coventry Street, is the **Wing Yip**, with another fine selection of oriental delights.

Health food – beyond lots and lots of lovely fresh fruit and veg – is catered for by ever-increasing outlets throughout the region. Within Birmingham, try the shop at **Friends of the Earth** at 54 Allison Street, Digbeth; the **Health Food Centre**, deep within the inner sanctum of the Bull Ring; **Natural World** in Bearwood Road, Bearwood; **Sage** in Alcester Road, Moseley. There *is* an alternative to Holland & Barratt.

Factory Shops

For real bargains, factory shops – where you can often pick up slight seconds and there is no 'middleman' – can be worth a good hike. The most notable area in Birmingham is the **Jewellery Quarter** (see *JOY RIDES*), and in the Black Country, the glassworks in and around **Stourbridge**. Seven miles from there is **Kidderminster**, said once to be the carpet capital of the world. Many of the surviving factories have shops and tours of cheap carpets, as well as the Kidderminster Carpet Auctions on Thursday, at the Retail Market on Comberton Hill, almost next to the twin railway stations. Trains half-hourly from Birmingham and Stourbridge, or buses down the A456.

Details of all the region's factory shops can be obtained from the excellent and informative *Factory Shop Guide: Western Midlands* by Gillian Cutress and Rolf Stricker, available at £2.95.

THE BLACK COUNTRY

Sitting in most 'booziz' in the Black Country, you will hear talk of 'gooin' oop Merry 'ill'. This is not a quaint local declaration of the speaker's state of mind – it refers, in fact, to the spanking new **Merry Hill Centre** in Brierley Hill (midway between Dudley and Stourbridge), served by copious numbers of buses from all over the region. A free mini-bus operates from many local centres. Occasionally more appropriately known as 'Merry Hell', the centre offers lots of colour-coded car parks (and lots of opportunity to watch dazed shoppers trying to remember which one they left the family Fiesta in), as well as a nifty monorail service whizzing you effortlessly from one corner of the empire to another.

Almost needless to say, you will find a comprehensive range of over 250 bright, climactically perfect and ultra-modern High Street stores, the odd fountain, a few 'scenic lifts' and lots of escalators. Opening hours are 1000-2000 Monday, Tuesday, Wednesday and Friday, 1000-2100 Thursday and 0900-1900 Saturday. And it's only Stage One that is complete.... Under discussion and planning at the moment is the tallest tower in the world (2,000 feet), complete with revolving restaurant and nightclub. There'll also be a waterfront Marina development for offices, a smattering of posh housing, a top hotel (who wants to stay in a shopping centre?), maybe a canal link to Dudley and the Black Country Museum, but – most importantly – yet More shops taking yet More credit cards from yet More over-consumerized, hypnotized robots.

It is hard to see which stores could possibly be missing from Merry Hill: there's the predictable crowd of BHS, C&A, WHS, M&S, B&Q, MFI, plus stores covering every rapid eye movement of the American Dream: soon to arrive Denture-U-Like or Kondom Korna. There are a handful of so-called speciality shops, but these tend to be in the rather more conservative and upmarket range.

Like all ultra-modern shopping developments, however, Merry Hill does offer an environment that is both hugely convenient and safe (but not for your credit card). Here you can eat, drink, park, use the entertainments laid on for kids, or the free wheelchair service and courtesy bus. It is overwhelmingly impressive, and mind-blowingly large . The Richardson brothers, who built the place on the site of the old Round Oak Steel Works, have defied the sceptics and, in doing so, have made themselves a wee bit of extra pocket money. It most certainly can be done.

Since its opening, Merry Hill has taken a growing slice of trade from local shopping areas, notably the hitherto traditional town centres of Dudley, Halesowen and Stourbridge. A wander around the **Churchill Precinct** in **Dudley** reveals a proliferation of empty shop windows adorned with forlorn signs proclaiming 'We have moved to Merry Hill'. Nonetheless, Dudley still has quite a lively, spacious and interesting centre that is a pleasure to stroll around, especially its excellent daily **market**, selling all kinds of food, clothes and householdy things. **Stourbridge** and **Halesowen** remain the kind of shopping centres that will service your daily needs, while failing to set your heart a-racing with trembling excitement.

A little farther away from the spreading tentacles of Merry Hill is **West Bromwich**, crowned by the **Sandwell Centre** around the High Street and King's and Queen's Squares. Covered precinct, all the shops you'd expect, very few of the ones you wouldn't. Need I say more? West Brom's markets are not as gargantuan as some of the near-neighbours, but can still be worth a browse. The High Street open market (household, food and rather nasty clothes) is on a Wednesday and Saturday; the under-cover market (more permanent stuff) is daily, except Tuesday.

Farther still (and the quality of the shops improves) is **Walsall** town centre. Here is one of the few places where you can still see the town's staple industries represented in the town centre shops. Like so many other West Midland towns, Walsall's market is its most interesting shopping feature – especially for the cheap china, pottery and crockery. The market is open on Monday, Tuesday, Thursday, Friday and Saturday, and is in Digbeth. Also of note is the **Walsall Antiques Centre** at 7a The Arcade (entrance from Digbeth arcade), housing dozens of antique dealers. The two precincts on offer are the **Old Square Shopping Centre** and the **Saddlers Centre**, both in the heart of town. Both have undergone 'extensive refurbishment', so you know what to expect.

Other interesting Black Country markets are: **Wednesbury** – bric-à-brac (and junk) on Tuesday, a general market on Friday and Saturday, and **Bilston**, with its antique market on Monday, Friday and Saturday in the High Street. Just about every other neighbourhood in the area (e.g. Tipton, Wednesfield, Cradley Heath, Blackheath, Brierley Hill (daily), Smethwick and Oldbury) has very general markets on various days of the week – nearly always including Saturday.

WOLVERHAMPTON

The centre of this town of over 200,000 inhabitants is functional. It is not especially beautiful, being perhaps one of the most striking examples of municipal shopping centre uniformity in Britain. If you closed your eyes and pictured an imaginary 'typical' shopping centre, you would come pretty close to imagining Wolverhampton. However, who needs aesthetics when you're buying undies? And buying undies is something that you can do a great deal of in this town because, quite simply, there are a lot of shops.

The two pedestrianized centres are unremarkable in the extreme: the **Wulfrun Centre** is either heart-stoppingly ugly or a magnificent example of late 1960s architecture, depending on your stand in the Great Prince Charles Architecture Debate. The neighbouring **Mander Centre** attempts to be considerably more upmarket by installing glitzy outdoor lifts and mirrors peeking out from behind mountains of plastic foliage. The two centres combined offer a remarkably unspectacular collection of shops of all sizes – all the major chains are here, coupled with a seemingly extortionate number of **Supercigs** branches. On the other side of life, **Rosemary Health Foods**, on the ground floor of the Mander Centre, is a large and well-laid-out store. Also in the Mander Centre is the **Wolverhampton Information Centre**, offering an excellent service aimed as equally at local residents as it is at visitors.

Car-parking facilities are good, and the two centres, coupled with the pedestrianized streets surrounding them, provide a solid selection of most of the chains and smaller shops that you are likely to need.

Pride of the new Wolverhampton is supposed to be the revamped and car-free **King Street**. What could have been a really interesting series of speciality shops has become little more than a collection of twee, potpourri-filled, flouncy, frilly mock olde worlde emporia. Kitsch gift shops, twinky cafés and exquisitely recreated Victoriana characterize the street at present.

Bookland and Company is – not surprisingly – a bookshop, perhaps Wolverhampton's best. They are at 65 Queen Street. The town's major department store is **Beatties**, on Victoria Street – a latter-day version of Grace Brothers. However, the store is gradually dragging itself into the latter half of the twentieth century. Catch it before the individuality disappears.

Sport

While Birmingham has not enjoyed recognition as the 'European City of Culture' (as has Glasgow), the second city quietly achieves and excels in other areas. Not least of these is Birmingham's title of **European City of Sport for All** for 1990-91, voted by the International Assembly of National Organizations of sport. And, indeed, a closer look at the city and region does show evidence of some steadily expanding facilities, not only for the sporting participant, but for spectators hungry to witness some of the best competition in the world.

This book can only scratch the surface of the wide and varied sporting scene – slug-racers and wellie-wangers may have to look elsewhere. What this section hopes to do is to direct those interested in 'mainstream' sports to be able to pursue them as a spectator or player.

SPORT AS A PARTICIPANT

There are a good many general facilities in the West Midlands, encompassing many indoor sports. The best way to find your nearest is to look under your local council's entry in the telephone directory. Such centres usually run general ongoing sports (e.g. badminton, squash, gym training, soccer etc.) as well as courses acording to demand (e.g. aerobics, judo, keep fit, karate to name but a few). Some eminently notable public sports centres in the region are:

Birmingham Sports Centre, just off the Middle Ring Road in Highgate (021-440 1021). A conspicuously located and well-used centre, whose astroturf pitch and swaggering facilities are clearly visible as you trundle along the ring road or the Balsall Heath Road. The centre has two main sports halls for badminton, volleyball, basketball, football, netball and cricket; an Olympic-standard gymnasium (not likely to see many Olympics in it, mind you...); a multi-purpose dividable room suitable for combat sports and some ball games; two matted fitness rooms for keep-fit, judo, wrestling and other combat sports/ball games; a multi-purpose gymnasium and outdoor tennis courts. BSC has a full timetable of instructed classes (daytime and evening), and welcomes all of any age (two upwards), ability or experience. Classes for women are held, and a crèche is operated on Tuesday, Wednesday and Thursday mornings. The centre also houses affiliated clubs in various sports, and an ever-increasing number of special events. One of the best-equipped sports facilities in the region, and well worth a look.

Hadley Stadium in Waterloo Road, Smethwick (021-420 2002) is on a far smaller scale than the Birmingham Sports Centre, but, probably as a result, there is a far stronger sense of community here. It's an excellent complex, with the best features being the floodlit outdoor hockey pitch, runnning track and well-lit indoor sports hall. The booking system is a little eccentric, but bear with it. Check with reception for details of events and clubs that run all year round from the stadium.

Laurel Road Sports & Social Club in Laurel Road, Handsworth (021-554 6712), belies the area's gaudy and undeserved reputation as a haven for every miscreant in town. It is a successful and very community-based club in a tranquil setting. Facilties include hard and grass tennis courts, a bowling green, cricket nets, football and hockey pitches – all being floodlit. An indoor area accommodates keep-fit classes, aerobics and table tennis. The centre feels unique with its combination of highly professional management and very welcoming and informal treatment. The grass courts are for serious players only, so don't stomp on with your old Ilie Nastase racquet and that mouldy old ball you found down the back of the sofa.

Other major centres meriting a mention are **Cocks Moors Woods** (in Alcester Road South, King's Heath, 021-444 8201), including a leisure pool, circuit-training facilities and an indoor hall for badminton, 5-a-side soccer and table tennis. **Harry Mitchell Sports Centre** (in Broomfield, Smethwick, 021-558 2973) is particularly noted for its outstanding squash facilities.

The Dell athletics stadium in Bryce Road, Pensnett near Dudley, has an all-weather athletics track and facilities for field sports, tennis, netball, football and bowling (0384-453514).

These represent but a tiny cross-section of existing centres in the region. One that is yet to be finished is the community hall linked to the burgeoning **National Indoor Sports Arena**, next to the International Convention Centre in Birmingham city centre's Broad Street. This will contain a double-court sports hall (a vast 72.5 metres long), enabling not only the usual sports to take place (including non-court marking activities such as gymnastics, trampolining, karate etc.), but also for it to serve as an athletic training/warm-up facility, which will be a first for Brum. The community hall will be primarily open for public use (along the lines of any other leisure/sports centre), although, on occasion, it will become the warm-up place for major events in the main arena. As a result, it will be a community hall with fantastically high standards, laid with a uniturf surface durable to withstand spikes. Can hardly wait, eh?

Snowy slopes are a little hard to find in the region, although there are some artifical **ski-slopes** in the new town of **Telford** (0952-680291) and one within the grounds of the hugely impressive **Ackers Trust** in Golden Hillock Road, Small Heath (021-771 4448). The Trust is a registered charity, promoting all manner of sporting challenges for people of all abilities, finances and skills on their 80-acre site. Apart from skiing, you can turn your hand to canoeing, kayaking, abseiling, orienteering, mountain biking, climbing or messing around on the canal. You can hire the ski-slope for a party, or a narrowboat for a residential trip, as well as be trained in any of the disciplines offered. The place has to be seen. Access and facilities for people with disabilities is excellent.

For sporting pursuits of a more rolling kind, the self-explanatory **Birmingham Wheels Park** on Adderley Road South, Bordesley, East Birmingham (near Adderley Park station). They offer BMX, motocross, stock car racing, roller speed skating and others, with equipment to be hired. Details on 021-771 2167.

Ice-skating took a knock when the Silver Blades rink in central Birmingham closed recently. The major remaining rink is at **Solihull**, in Hobs Moat Road, Olton (021-742 5561). Open every afternoon and most mornings and evenings. They hold learn-to-skate courses, and host the Solihull Barons ice hockey team on Sunday evenings during the season.

More information about facilties or sports coaching can be obtained from the **West Midland region of the Sports Council** at Metropolitan House, Hagley Road, Five Ways B16 8TT (021-456 3444). For details of council facilties, contact your local borough council (addresses and numbers in *THE POTTED WEST MIDLANDS*). All councils offer discount sports and leisure packages to the unemployed, those on income support, over-sixty (and not working), full-time students, ET or YTS trainees or people with disabilities. Why pay the full rate for things such as swimming, bowls, fishing, tennis, squash, badminton, sauna, athletics or golf if you don't have to? The **British Sports Association for the Disabled** have a regional office in Birmingham, which can be contacted on 021-354 5369.

For more intensive pursuit of particular sports, the best approach is to contact the relevant sports association(s), most having branches in the West Midlands. These can be found in the phone directory, or enquire at the regional Sports Council.

Some sports are a little harder to track down than others. The martial arts schools, for instance, are a paricularly 'secret society', even though there is plenty of healthy activity going on. A useful source of information is Ray Jewel at the **Birmingham City Martial Arts centre** (021-643 2178), who also run regular exhibitions at the **Castle Vale Leisure Centre**, open to all ages. Other highly recommended schools include the **Codrington Budokan Martial Arts & Fitness Studio** (021-622 3737), the **Shukokai Karate Centre** (021-643 3964) and **Temple Karate** (021-643 1759).

If fighting at a more Neanderthal level is your thing, **boxing** is alive and kicking, with approximately forty clubs operating in the area. The West Midlands boxing secretary can be reached on 021-443 1759 for a wealth of pugilistic knowledge and directions to your nearest fistic fraternity.

On a far more sedate note, a very accessible pastime is **swimming**. Nowhere in the region is far from a pool, although quite a few are relics from a Victorian public slipper bath. Modern and bright pools (such as at **Sparkhill**) extend to gym and sauna facilties too.

Tennis is generally poorly dealt with, the West Midlands seeming just as uninterested in producing an international champion as is the rest of Britain. If you cannot afford the often prohibitive cost of joining a very good club, you can only rely on public parks, few among which provide a decent standard of court (**Cannon Hill park** being a notable exception), and all of which charge twice the hourly rate should you have the audacity to play doubles. If you can afford the arm and a leg, **Aston Lesiure Centre** have some beautiful indoor courts, and if you want to pretend you're on Centre Court by playing on grass, **King's Heath** have some courts that are more reminiscent of a very outside court. If you actually want to try tournament play, contact your nearest Lawn Tennis Association for details of the Volkswagen ratings tournaments, held each year and giving you the chance to compete at your own level in as many competitions as you can handle. You don't need to be a club member to take part.

There are a considerable number of public **golf** courses, where you don't have to buy thousands of pounds worth of equipment to strut around the 18 holes, as you can hire the clubs. Try the courses at **Cocks Moor Woods**, King's Heath (021-444 3584) and **Hatchford Brook**, Coventry Road –where you can get a bit of plane-spotting in as well, being next to the airport (021-743 9821).

Indoor **bowling** has come back as an immensely popular Friday night activity that can be loosely classified as a sport. In Pershore Street, Brum city centre, the old Silver Blades ice rink has transmogrified into the **GX Superbowl** (021-666 7525). In the southern swathe of the city, there is also the **Stirchley Superbowl** on the Pershore Road (021-458 4444) and the **Acocks Green Bowling Alley** in Westley Road (021-706 1669).

Cycling is not only a economical and enviromentally-chummy means of transport, but also one of the most accessible and healthy activities around. See *Travel and Transport* in *ORIENTATION*.

SPORT AS A SPECTATOR

Not even Birmingham's mother was really surprised that she failed to win the 1992 Olympic bid. The effort, however, did highlight the region's capability as a rostrum for international sport. Major events that occur annually in the city at present are:

- March: **'Champions All'** national gymnastics championships (National Exhibition Centre). NEC Box Office: 021-780 4133.
- May: the Carlsberg **National Basketball Championships** (NEC)
- June: the pre-Wimbledon **Dow Classic** ladies tennis tournament (Edgbaston Priory), which attracts most of the top names. Details on 021-440 2492.
- Summer: International cricket **test matches** at the Warwickshire County Ground at Edgbaston. Details on 021-446 4422.
- June: the **Royal International Horse Show** (NEC)
- August Bank Holiday: the **Birmingham Super prix** road race: rather like having nest of amorous hornets in your brain for two days if you live locally. See *JOY RIDES*. Details on 021-235 2026.

Recent one-off events at the NEC have included the European Figure Skating Championships and the demolition of Black Country boxing hero Pat Cowdell in a losing world-title contest.

The **Alexander Stadium** in Perry Park, sandwiched between the M6 and the A34 Walsall road in Perry Barr, hosts major athletics events throughout the sporting year. Details of the big names and gabbling commentators on 021-356 8008.

On the main railway line between Wolverhampton and Telford, the athletics stadium at **RAF Cosford** hosts many national and international indoor track and field events. Details on 0902-372393.

Needless to say, **football** enjoys healthy support in the region, even if some of the clubs are a little sickly. Nigel Kennedy's **Aston Villa** (Villa Park 021-327 6604) are current torch-bearers for Midlands' soccer in Barclays League Division one after their (not quite so) near-miss in the 1989/90 championship race. **West Bromwich Albion** (The Hawthorns 021-525 8888) and **Wolverhampton Wanderers** (Molineux 0902-712181/27524) are both lurching along, Wolves having had an especially good time in the past few years after their 1980s doldrums. That leaves sorry old **Birmingham City** (St Andrew's 021-772 2689), ancient enemies of Villa, but now about as much of a threat as a toothless guinea-pig as they face such inspirational opposition as Chester, Cambridge or Brentford. Last – and, sadly, least – are **Walsall** (Fellowes Park 0922-22791), slowly decomposing in Division Four. The city's only top-flight **Rugby Union** club is the old red-and-black **Moseley** (The Reddings 021-449 2149).

The major **cricket** ground is the Warwickshire County Ground, on the B4217 Edgbaston Road in sunny **Edgbaston**. As well as being able to watch the ups and downs of the county side, a number of Test Matches are played here. Buses 45/7 from Corporation Street, 61/2/3 from Colmore Row or 1 from Five Ways. Details on 021-446 4422.

A sporting night out with a slight difference can be had at the **Hall Green Dog Track** (York Road, 021-777 1181). As well as the chance to watch lithe greyhounds belting after a mechanical hare, there is a fine selection of eateries and watering holes. Train to Hall Green station, or No.11 bus. **Speedway** is big in the region, with tracks at **Wolverhampton** (Sutherland Avenue, Monmore Green, 0902-870400) and **Cradley Heath** (Dudley Wood Road, 0384-69008), home of the top-class Heathens. **Horse-racing** on the flat at **Wolverhampton** racecourse (0902-24481).

The new **National Indoor Arena** is already bidding to hold future top-class events. The six-lane 200-metre athletics track is unique in Britain in being movable, thus leaving an immense floor space that can be adapted for any indoor sport. Even ice events will be possible (very necessary after the sad demise of Silver Blades) at the arena, which claims to be 'the facility for which Birmingham and the UK have long been waiting'. Maybe not when you see your poll-tax bill ....

8. THE MORAL MAJORITY

This chapter is intended to paint a brief portrait of the amenities and resources available for sections of society that, by and large, get a bum deal more often than most. It is not meant to be patronizing in throwing them all in together, especially as it should be borne in mind – as suggested by the chapter title – that the people who are being addressed cover about three-quarters of the population of the West Midlands!

Naturally, the sections which follow interrelate with much else in the book. However, the attempt here is to clear away some of the extraneous information to enable you to focus on specific groups of people.

Women's Organizations and Facilities in the West Midlands

This brief section is intended to give an initial idea of the hundreds of groups and services that are particularly available to women throughout the region. The vast range of relevant organizations means that this can only skim the surface: it is intended to cover a few local groups, events and organizations that are fundamentally aimed only at women. Some women-only and lesbian entries are in the *Lesbian and Gay* section.

There is quite a high level of activity going on that is geared towards the needs of women in the West Midlands. All local councils have made some kind of commitment to pursuing an equal opportunities policy, although the implementation of this can be enacted in just about any way from very thorough to utterly lethargic. The whole range is evident in even the small number of authorities under scrutiny here.

Birmingham City Council, as by far the largest and the wealthiest, made the commitment to financing an excellent full-time **Women's Unit**, which is a very informative and helpful resource for all. The most public and upfront realization of their work is the annual **Women's Festival** in March. This brings together dozens of groups and events into a co-ordinated structure – covering the arts, education, sport, health, politics and discussion.

CONTACTS

Asian Women's Centre: 021-523 0109.
Birmingham City Council Women's Unit: 021-235 4466.
Birmingham Rape Crisis and Research Centre at PO Box 558, Birmingham B3 2HL, 021-233 2122 (counselling) or 021-233 2655 (office).
Birmingham Women's Advice & Information Centre: a brilliant phone- or drop-in resource to point you in the right direction for all kinds of information. Partially wheelchair accessible – phone in advance. At 15a Devonshire House, High Street, Digbeth B12 0LP, 021-773 6952.
Citizens' Advice Bureau: help and advice on matters legal, practical or financial. See phone book for details.
Dudley Council Community Development Unit (including Equal Opportunities): 0384-453181.
Second Sight: women's co-operative video training and production company offering courses and instruction. At Zair Works, 111 Bishop Street, Birmingham B5 6JL, 021-622 5750.
Wolverhampton Council Equal Opportunities Unit: 0902-27811.
Wolverhampton Rape Crisis: 21 Temple Street, 0902-27223.
Wolverhampton Well Women's Advice & Information Centre: covers all areas of health. Crèche and wheelchair-accessible. At 10 King Street, Wolverhampton, WV1 1ST, 0902-29217.
Women's Workshops Ltd.: 021-773 5511.
Women's Therapy Centre: 43 Ladywood Middleway, Birmingham B16 8HA, 021-455 8677.

The Birmingham City Council Women's Unit are currently working on a *Women's Directory*, to be published in 1991. There will be a small charge for this, the aim of which is to give women across the city a central resource covering many aspects of their lives. It should be available through libraries, neighbourhood centres and council offices. Ring the unit for details.

Black and Ethnic

The West Midlands is a long-established, and largely proud, multi-racial area. Racism undoubtedly exists, but the spectre of it is not as acute as in many other parts of Britain. Of course, there have been events such as the 1985 disturbances in Handsworth and the sporadic strong presence of far-Right groups such as the National Front and the British

National Party, but incidences of these kinds are fewer than many conurbations experience.

Some of the most flagrant instances of racism come in the daily channels of housing, employment and nightlife. Concerning the latter, ever since the 1974 Birmingham pub bombings, many city centre pubs and clubs have operated a strict door policy – frequently little more than thinly veiled anti-Black or anti-Irish racism. The policy of employing bouncers has increased throughout the 1980s, as establishments decide to magically zap themselves upmarket by placing a couple of pea-brained big bigots on the door. Recently the *Sunday Correspondent* succeeded in getting White journalists into certain clubs where Black journalists had just failed to gain entry. The local **Commission for Racial Equality** (CRE) say that such problems are commonplace, and that about one-third of the 250-odd complaints that they receive annually concern racism in nightclub door policies.

If you do come across – or are subjected to – incidences of racism or harassment, contact the regional office of the CRE in Birmingham. They can provide help and guidance with legal and practical matters, and are found at Alpha Tower, Suffolk Street, Queensway, Birmingham B1 1TT (021-632 4544). For people of any ethnic origin, the CRE can be a very useful first port of call.

A further recent innovation is the launch of the **Birmingham Racial Attacks Monitoring Unit**, based at the **Afro-Caribbean Resource Centre**, 339 Dudley Road, Winson Green B18 4HB (021-454 9500). They aim to offer support, help and advice for those who have suffered from racially motivated attacks, as well as working to gain greater police and public recognition of this crime and to campaign for changes in the law. The **Wolverhampton Afro-Caribbean Development Agency** is at 52 Worcester Street, Wolverhampton (0902-24005).

The West Midlands **Asian Resource Centre** is nearby at 101 Villa Road, Handsworth, Birmingham B19 1NH (021-551 4518 or 021-523 0580) for advice, support and information. Wolverhampton's **Surdhwani** society for the promotion of Asian arts and culture can be contacted on 0902-32375.

Local **Community Relations Councils** act as overseers of local policy and good practice in all walks of life. They have considerable sway with statutory authorities. The Birmingham branch is at 32-34 Hill Street (021-235 4309), while for the Black Country, contact 2 Clarence Road, Wolverhampton (0902-713629 or 773580).

Most of the local councils have equal-opportunities sections, or staff devoted to the implementation of their policy. Birmingham City Council is the only one with a specific **Race Relations Unit**, which is on 021-235 2545.

Black and ethnic arts in the West Midlands are thriving. The **West Midlands Ethnic Minority Arts Service** (WEMAS), an independent charity, acts as a co-ordinator for many of the Arts events in the area for the Black and ethnic community. They maintain a register of local artists and produce an annual *Black Artist's Creative Handbook* for the West Midlands. It costs nothing to register for their directory, although a fiver will guarantee you a space in the handbook, as well as four laser-printed CVs.

They are also seeking volunteers who may be between jobs and could give a hand in getting mailings despatched. WEMAS bring out a bi-monthly *Bulletin*, giving a comprehensive run down of events (including dance, cabaret, theatre, art, film and photography), as well as news, reviews and listings. The *Bulletin* is free, and is widely available around arts venues, libraries and Black centres. Find out more from WEMAS at 23 Hamstead Road, Handsworth, Birmingham B19 1BX, (021-507 1262).

One of the area's premier predominantly Afro-Caribbean venues is **The Cave** at 516 Moseley Road, Balsall Heath (021-440 3742) – buses 50, 177/8/9. Here you can see and hear dance, theatre and music (including bhangra events), or get involved with some of the groups working from here.

Arts events and festivals take place throughout the year – from the renowned and ebullient **Handsworth Carnival** to a brand-new **Afrikan Music Festival** at the Muhammed Ali Centre in Hockley's Icknield Street (021-554 7248). Arts companies have emerged in recent years – look out for the nationally acclaimed local African/Caribbean dance company **Kokuma**.

The **Harambee** organization in Grove Lane, just off the Soho Road in central Handsworths is a Black community group, offering all kinds of help, information and advice (021-554 8479). They are next door to the redoubtable **Hareriet Tubman** bookshop. Buses 74/6/8/9.

The area's large **Irish** population is served well by the **Irish Welfare and Information Centre** at Plunkett House, Shadwell Street, Birmingham B4 6EU (behind St Chad's catholic cathedral in the city centre), 021-233 2754/236 9312. The city's main **Irish Community Centre** is in Digbeth High Street (021- 622 2314/2322).

People with Disabilities

In recent years, awareness of the many needs of people with disabilities has risen, and forced all kinds of companies, organizations and groups to reassess their service or provision. This section can only hope to scratch the surface of the multifarious groups in the region that are working to promote the needs and opportunities of people with a vast range of differing disabilities.

GROUPS AND ORGANIZATIONS FOR PEOPLE WITH DISABILITIES:

The **West Midlands Council for Disabled People** covers the West Midlands county and the surrounding region, and their Information Office is the first port of call for all enquiries concerning local groups, facilities and amenities. They produce a quarterly magazine, *Pinpoint*, covering a multitude of topics, from fashion to politics, transport to books. They are at the Moseley Hall Hospital, Birmingham B13 8JL (021-449 1225).

The **Birmingham Disability Rights** (021-359 6337) group campaigns for a greater political awareness and action to equalize the opportunities for the 90,000-plus people with disabilties throughout the region.

Access for All is an organization working to promote involvement in all kinds of access issues (not just physical access) for individuals, operating within Birmingham. They are currently working to produce a comprehensive and free access guide to public amenities (including shops and transport) within the West Midlands, which will be available for visitors and residents alike. They are based in the beautiful old Curzon Street station building at 1 Curzon Street, Birmingham B4 7XG (021-359 0654). They also produce a quarterly magazine that is totally different to the factual *Pinpoint*. AfA's *Spotlight* (including *Spotlight for Youth)* is an enjoyable and informative read that covers more topics in one issue than all the Sunday supplements put together. And it's a lot funnier.... The Midlands' **Resource Centre for Deaf People** is at 4 Church Road, Edgbaston B15 3TD (021-454 9991).

A recent and very welcome innovation has been to produce an excellent and clear summary of access to many public buildings in the front of the Birmingham **telephone directory**. The venues covered spread into the Black Country, and give information on the distance from parking, the gradient of the entrance, whether there's a lift, adapted toilets, an induction loop, an accessible bar/restaurant and help available at a load of cinemas, theatres, museums, concert venues and transport centres throughout the area. It's an excellent innovation, and one that it is hoped will be expanded.

Transport is a particularly thorny area for those with access problems. The West Midlands sadly over-depends on buses for its public transport, which presents some of the most difficult problems for people with disabilties. The passenger transport executive, CENTRO, produce a very thorough book (available free) called *Getting Around* which covers a huge range of detail, especially for the local rail network. For all enquiries, telephone the Centro Hotline on 021-200 2700. The service has a Minicom V TDD machine to aid those with hearing or speech difficulty. A Ring and Ride minibus service is available in most parts of the region: details from the **West Midlands Special Needs Transport**, who are at 206-212 Windsor Street, Nechells, Birmingham, B7 4NE (021-333 3107). This is also the home of the **National Advisory Unit for Accessible Transport**, who can be reached at the same address, or on 021-333 3105. If you're venturing further afield, free advice on planning any journey throughout the UK can be obtained from **Tripscope** at 63 Esmond Road, London W4 1JE (081-994 9294).

West Midlands Arts have considerable input from people with disabilties for their many activities in co-ordinating events right across the spectrum. They are great for information and ideas – contact them at 82 Granville Street (between Broad Street and Bath Row) in the city centre (021-631 3121).

Shopmobility schemes are in operation for those who have problems getting around the bargains. One of the best is operated at the **Merry Hill Centre** in Brierley Hill (details on 0384-481141, Extension 25). Others operate in Sandwell and Sutton Coldfield. An information centre and shop for people with disabilties is in the pipeline for Birmingham city centre.

The local authorities in the area all provide support, advice and information for all sections of the community. Telephone your local town hall or council offices for more information on what you're getting for your poll-tax. Contact numbers and addresses in *THE POTTED WEST MIDLANDS*.

The Lesbian and Gay West Midlands

A virulently right-wing American observer recently made the wild claim that the streets of Birmingham were full of flaunting gays. I don't know when she was there, but it's not a common perception. In actual fact, the range of amenities for the lesbian and gay population is not anywhere near as broad as you might perhaps expect in a conurbation of two million lost souls.

Central Birmingham has the greatest concentration of things to keep you occupied, although, as is so common right across the country, most of the places are very much orientated towards gay men. As ever, lesbians tend to get a bit of a naff deal.

CLUBS AND PUBS

Most are situated in Birmingham city centre. The **Nightingale Club** at 40 Thorpe Street (behind the Hippodrome) is the main venue, open every night until 2000 (midnight on Sundays). Drag acts, disco, restaurant, theme nights and four bars – however, a conservative guess by someone working there that it is ninety per cent men underlines the problem. Similarly, **The Jug** club at 27 Water Street, the other side of the ring road from Snow Hill station, won't admit women unless accompanied by a (male) member. Discos most nights till late.

Peacocks at the New Imperial Hotel in Temple Street (entrance via Needless Alley) is far more mixed and very popular. They have regular entertainment (mainly discos), including a women-only disco on the last Saturday of each month upstairs in the Connaught Room. The tackily named **Partners** in Hurst Street has weekend discos, weekday quizzes, films and discos and cabaret/drag on Sunday evenings. For the most clone-like experience, drag your handlebar moustache and check shirt along to **Jesters** at Holloway Circus Queensway. A more mixed and generally far less cloney crowd use the back bar at the **Queen Victoria** pub in John Bright Street, behind the Alexandra theatre. Popular at weekends, often having live music. Brand-new two-floor club **Tin Tin's** at 308 Bull Ring Centre, Smallbrook Queensway (021-643 4129) is a very welcome addition to the rather enclosed scene in the city. Operating from Tuesday through to Sunday, this is rapidly becoming *the* place to drink, dance and eat.

In Wolverhampton, the **Greyhound** pub in Bond Street is a friendly, mixed pub that is gay mainly in the lounge bar. For a spot of funking, the **Silver Web** club in Whitmore Street (near the station) has mixed gay nights on Tuesday, Friday and Saturday until 0230, women's night on Thursday. For the slightly cruisier side of life **Gavan's Club** in Darlington Street (entrance on Clarence Street) is a disco and drag club open from Tuesday to Saturday.

The **Station** in King's Heath High Street (021-444 1257) hosts a women-only bar and disco every Tuesday night. Up towards town, in Tindall Street, Balsall Heath (021-440 1954) is the **Old Moseley**, which isn't a 'certified' l&g pub, but does attract quite a mixed clientele and can be worth a good evening.

Walsall's only gay pub is the M&B **Golden Lion** in Birchills Street, Birchills, by the Walsall locks. Boasting a very camp decor, the Lion hosts weekend discos. Entrance is not for the faint-hearted – although it's very friendly and open, you have to ring the doorbell first!

OTHER AMENITIES

In the Pink is the title of the monthly free newspaper for lesbians and gay men in the West Midlands. The collective who publish it are contactable at 37 Thorp Street, Birmingham B5 4AU. It's obtainable through many of the gay outlets and at **Key Books**, Brum's only real radical bookshop (which stocks lots of other lesbian and gay interest literature) at 136 Digbeth. They also stock *Scene Out* magazine which, although proclaiming itself as the mouthpiece of 'the Lesbian and Gay North' covers the Midlands pretty well. These two – plus the indispensable *Gay Times*, available throughout the region, even if you still have to stretch towards the top shelf in the newsagent's – cover most of the special-interest lesbian and gay groups in the region. Details of regular gay men's and lesbians' social or political groups can be obtained either from the **West Midlands Lesbian & Gay Switchboard** from 0700-2000 daily on 021-622 6589 (or the national 24-hour switchboard in London on 071-837 7324). The Birmingham **Lesbian Line** is on 021-773 5310 from 1930-2100 on Wednesdays (London line 071-251 6911 from 1400-2000, Monday and Friday and 1900-2000 Tuesday to Thursday). **West Midland Friend** provides help and counselling for all lesbians, gays, bisexuals and their families on 021-622 7351.

The gay store **Clone Zone** has recently opened up at 42 Bristol Street, Birmingham (021-666 6640) for a fine selection of toys, games, erotic wear and other delights. The **Wolverhampton Lesbian, Gay and Bisexual Centre** is at 489 Willenhall Road, and hosts a weekly social from 1400-1700 on Saturdays and a discussion group every Wednesday at 2000. Ring WM Switchboard for further details. All of the **universities** and **polytechnics** in the region have regular lesbian and gay groups, many of which are open to non-students. More details from *Switchboard* or listings in the various magazines.

If you've got lots of people staying – or are looking for a short-term Midlands base yourself – the region's main **gay guest-house** is **Oakleaves** in Handsworth Wood. Incredibly friendly and resilient, having survived systematic persecution over years. If you go once, you will become a regular visitor, and friend (021-551 6510).

The Green West Midlands

O come all ye Ecover buyers, for in the West Midlands can ye find enough greenery to keep all happy. Yep, folks, environmental concerns have reached the region that most think is still one big black pit.

The region is, in fact, surprisingly full of lush green spaces, some of which are streets ahead of the packed green 'lungs' in cities such as London. More details in *JOY RIDES*.

The whole area defies all the grim, grey stereotypes. Community and voluntary groups are working with the councils in the area to make major strides to ensure that this little section of the nation has a far more pleasant environment. Even unlikely urban landscapes like the Birmingham Middle Ring Road are absolutely bursting with flowers for mile upon mile.

RECYCLING

No council would try and bamboozle its poll-tax payers by failing to provide an ever-increasing barrage of overflowing skips, grandiosely entitled Recycling Centres. Ring your local council to find the nearest one to accept your embarrassingly large empty bottle collection in the dead of night.

Many of these centres now have skips for waste paper. Alternatively, there are always legions of trusty little boys in woggles, the odd animal sanctuary and some schools and hospitals that take waste paper in bulk. Your council can advise. To buy the stuff back after it's been recycled is pretty easy too: most stationers (including W.H.Smith, Woolworths and Rymans) stock a plentiful supply of vastly overpriced recycled paper. Oxfam shops have a particularly good range, and at least you're not lining the pockets of some fat eco-exploiter.

Most household items can be recycled in some shape: aluminium cans (often at the same sites as Bottle Banks), car batteries and motor oil, clothing and furniture (charity shops or, if a little shabbier, a local jumble sale). A Friends of the Earth/*Daily Telegraph* initiative are their county-based recycling directories. The West Midlands directory is available from bookshops across the region, as well as the **Friends of the Earth** shop at 54, Allison Street in Digbeth, central Birmingham (021-632 6909). The FoE centre brings together all kinds of groups and resources of varying shades of green – from the excellent Amazon café to the cycling campaign group, Pushbikes. It's definitely the place to start your search for a better life.

For residents of Birmingham, there is also the excellent *Birmingham Green Guide*, produced by City Pack and selling at £4.95. This covers just about any area of eco-awareness, and gives reams of useful contacts..

LOCAL GROUPS AND ORGANIZATIONS

Birmingham for People sprung to prominence in recent years over discussions about the future of the city centre. While the profit-motivated planners would have razed the Bull Ring to build just a bigger shopping complex, this group successfully lobbied to put the everyday users of the city centre back on centre stage. They can be contacted c/o Birmingham Voluntary Services Council, 138 Digbeth, B5 6DR (021-643 4343).

Think Green is a national organization, based in Brum, campaigning for a steady greening of Britain's cities and towns. At Premier House, 43-48 New Street, Birmingham B2 4LJ (021-643 8899). An umbrella group for all those trying to make the land a little more green and pleasant is the **West Midlands Environment Network** at 3 Tower Street, Birmingham B19 3RL (021-359 3973). They are very helpful in putting you in touch with the group to service your needs. They also publish a monthly magazine, *Talking Green*, which has endless lists of talks, courses, walks, events and activities that should surely satiate your every environmental whim.

Voluntary Work

There are many different ways that you can put those armchair principles into action – whether for an environmental project or any one of hundreds of other organizations that are desperate for volunteer help. There is far more to volunteering than donning a twin-set, pearls and a sensible floral cardy in order to stand behind the counter at the local Oxfam shop.

Councils for Voluntary Service co-ordinate the work of volunteers and voluntary organizations throughout the region. They are able to give you copious ideas, details and contacts to fit in with the kind of work that you want to do, how much time you may have to spare and what your interests and skills are.

Birmingham Voluntary Service Council, is one of the largest and most impressive in the country. At 138 Digbeth, Birmingham B5 6DR (021-643 4343).

Conservation Volunteers in Firsby Road, Quinton (021-426 5588) is for all those who want to put in a good day's outdoor graft on a conservation project.

Dudley Council for Voluntary Service, 7 Albion Street, Brierley Hill (0384-73381/78166).

Walsall Guild for Voluntary Services, 50 Lower Hall Lane, Walsall (0922-38825).

Wolverhampton Voluntary Services Council, 2-3 Bell Street, Wolverhampton (0902-773761).

Birmingham University Community Action (ComAc) office (for Brum Uni students), Guild of Students, Edgbaston Park Road, Birmingham B15 2TU (021-472 1841).

Community Service Volunteers are people aged 18-35 involved with a vast range of voluntary projects. Find out more from CSV, St Peter's Urban Village Trust, College Road, Saltley B8 3TE (021-327 1351).

Adult and Continuing Education

One of the most rewarding and worthwhile ways of spending a bit of your precious spare time is in taking on some classes. These can range from an hour a week flower-arranging in the local community centre to a correspondence degree course. The list of places that provide such courses is almost endless, but this section will hopefully prod you in some of the right directions.

The **Workers' Educational Association** is big round here, as is the range of courses and projects that they offer. School governor training, Black women's history, local history, quantum theory for beginners (sic), the art of classical Greece, herbs and their uses – these are all (genuine) recent WEA courses held in the West Midlands. For details of their activities, contact the District Office at 78-80 Sherlock Street, Birmingham B5 6LT (021-666 6101).

All local councils run evening and day release courses at local schools and colleges – details are far too many to go into here. The higher-education establishments – especially the Polytechnics in Birmingham and Wolverhampton – also run many courses, right up to higher degree level. Wolverhampton Poly has a particularly good record of community involvement, as can be witnessed in their **Higher Education Shop** at 62-64 Lichfield Street in the town centre.

The **Brasshouse Centre** at 50 Sheepcote Street (off Broad Street), in central Birmingham (021-643 0114) is the region's very impressive centre for languages. Whether it's elementary Japanese, intermediate Dutch or advanced Welsh, the Brasshouse can suit your need. There is a crèche and a cafeteria. Tuition fees vary from about £15 to £50 per term, with large concessions for Passport to Leisure and Learning cards.

9. THE POTTED WEST MIDLANDS

Tourist Information Centres

TICs are the best places to get a wide range of information about places, happenings, events, accommodation and all served with a dash of total enthusiasm.

2 City Arcade, **Birmingham** city centre, 021-643 2514.
The Piazza, **National Exhibition Centre**, 021-780 4321.
Central Library, Homer Road, **Solihull**, 021-704 6130.
Mander Centre, **Wolverhampton**, 0902-312051.
39 Churchill Precinct, **Dudley**, 0384-250333.
Library, Crown Centre, **Stourbridge**, 0384-394004.

Useful Contacts

LOCAL COUNCILS

Birmingham City Council: 021-235 9944.
Dudley Borough Council: 0384-456000.
Sandwell Borough Council: Town Hall, West Bromwich, 021-569 2200.
Solihull Borough Council: 021-704 6000.
Walsall Borough Council: 0922-650000.
Wolverhampton Borough Council: 0902-27811.

HELP AND ADVICE

AIDS Line: 021-622 1511.
AIDS Life Line & Counselling Centre (telephone and face-to-face): 021-235 3535, Monday-Friday 1000-1930.
National AIDS Line (free): 0800-567123.
Alcoholics Anonymous: 021-773 3449, 1900-2000 nightly.
Brook Advisory Centres (pregnancy tests, contraception supplies and information):
Birmingham City Centre: 021-643 5341
Saltley and E. Birmingham: 021-328 4544
Handsworth: 021-554 7553
Edgbaston: 021-455 0491.

Citizens Advice Bureaux (help with a vast range of legal, housing, work-related or any other problem):
All over the West Midlands: see phone directory for nearest.

Drug Line Counselling and Advice: 021-632 6363.
British Pregnancy Advisory Service: 021-643 1461.
Relate (relationship problems): 021-643 1638.
Samaritans (confidential advice lines):
Birmingham: 021-666 6644
Solihull: 021-704 2255
Brierley Hill: 0384-78111.
Young People's Advisory Service (general counselling and help): 021-643 0392.

DOCTORS AND NURSES

If you need a list of local doctors, reputable opticians and dentists, in order that you can choose whose hands you're going to put your life in, contact your local **Family Practitioner Committee**:

Birmingham: 021-333 4444
Wolverhampton: 0902-20281
Sandwell: 021-553 1774
Dudley: 0384-239376
Walsall: 0922-29861.

For the details of your nearest **Sexually Transmitted Diseases** or **Family Planning Clinic**, look in the phone book under the local Health Authority entry.

Homeopathy is gaining increasing respect across the board of medical opinion. Hundreds of thousands of people swear by it. Quite a lot of others think it's utter hocus pocus. If you decide to try a homeopath (and there are plenty advertising), check that they are legitimate and recognized by contacting your local Family Practitioner Committee (see above) or the Registered Society of Homeopaths on 021-443 6616.

INDEX

PUBS INDEX